THE SOCIETY OF PUBLICATION DESIGNERS 24TH PUBLICATION DESIGN ANNUAL

WATSON-GUPTILL PUBLICATIONS/NEW YORK

ACKNOWLEDGEMENTS

TWENTY-FOURTH PUBLICATION DESIGN ANNUAL

DESIGNERS

Anthony Russell

Samuel Kuo

Anthony Russell & Associates Inc.
New York, NY

TYPOGRAPHER

Phoenix Typographers, Inc.
Long Island, NY

COMPETITION CHAIRPERSONS

Derek Ungless

Robert Priest

CATEGORY CHAIRPERSONS

Melissa Tardiff

Bob Ciano

Phyllis Cox

John Belknap

EXHIBITION COMMITTEE

Nora Sheehan

CALL FOR ENTRIES CREDITS

Designed by

Derek Ungless

Robert Priest

Thanks to

Westvaco Corporation
New York, NY

Northeast Graphics
North Haven, CT

Anagraphics, Inc.
New York, NY

Type Consortium, Inc.
New York, NY

New York Times Foundation

SPECIAL THANKS TO

Paul Geczik

Andrea Cobb

Delgis Canahuate

Jennifer Wood

OFFICERS

President
Diana La Guardia
Condé Nast Traveler

Vice President
Derek Ungless
Vogue

Secretary
Amy Bogert
MS

Treasurer
Lee Ann Jaffee
Lee Ann Jaffee Design

BOARD OF DIRECTORS

Robert Altemus
Altemus Design

Roger Black
Roger Black, Inc.

John Belknap
7 Days

Tom Bentkowski
Life

Karen Bloom
Westvaco Corporation

Bob Ciano
Travel and Leisure

Phyllis Richmond Cox
Bride's

Virginia Smith
Baruch College

Melissa Tardiff
Town & Country

Mary Zisk
Creative Ideas

EXECUTIVE DIRECTOR

Bride M. Whelan

2

CONTENTS

INTRODUCTION TO SPD

The Society of Publication Designers meets the needs of editorial art directors and designers across the country. By encouraging a forum among the most accomplished professionals in the field, and by inviting the best of them to judge in competition each year, the Society promotes rigorous standards of achievement in publication design. SPD recognizes the art director in an editorial capacity, as a visual journalist, and honors those who distinguish themselves in this way.

A variety of activities are offered by the Society which include the yearly Competition, the Awards Gala, the Annual, and the Exhibition; a monthly Speaker's Evening brings together distinguished professionals to share their unique contributions to publication design: a bi-monthly newsletter, GRIDS, highlights activities and general information of the Society and the various goings-on amidst the publications community; and the SPOTS competition, for editorial illustrators.

The Society of Publication Designers, founded in 1965, is a non-profit organization.

E ach competition has its own personality—formed by its own unique
combination of judges and material
to be judged. This is certainly the case with
the 24th annual Society of Publication
Designers show, and on behalf of the board
I would like to thank again the judges from
all over Europe and the United States for
their painstaking effort.

The breadth of their judgments deserve
comment. Selected works range from gritty,
unadorned black-and-white photojournalism
to pristine, manicured and highly stylized
magazine art. Common to all of them,
though, is a conviction that content should
not be oppressed by overdesign, that ideas
and emotions are most powerful when com-
municated in a straightforward way.

It isn't luck that is celebrated here but
perseverance. The visual expression of editorial objectives depends on the collaboration
between art director and editor, and the suc-
cess of that collaboration depends on it beginning early on. Works cited demonstrate
the art directors' design skills but, as important, their ability to achieve a full and spir-
ited partnership in the editorial process.

BRIGITTE LACOMBE

5

Matt Mahurin
Photographer

Fabien Baron
Art Director
Italian Vogue

Fred Woodward
Art Director
Rolling Stone

Neville Brody
Principal
Neville Brody Design UK

Gregory Curtis
Editor
Texas Monthly

TRADE PUBLICATION *Left to Right*

Fausto Pellegrini
Art Director
Jan Krukowski Associates

Terry Koppel
Principal
Koppel & Scher

Richelle Huff
Art Director
Progressive Architecture

Will Hopkins
Partner
Hopkins/Baumann, Inc.

Henry Brimmer
Art Director
Photo Metro

CORPORATE PUBLICATION *Left to Right*

Pari Stave
Curator
Equitable Life Assurance Society

Louis Fishauf
Principal
Reactor Art & Design

Nancye L. Green
Partner
Donovan & Green

Michael Bierut
Vice President
Vignelli Associates

Michael Mabry
Principal
Michael Mabry Design

NEWSPAPER AND TABLOID *Left to Right*

Walter Bernard
Partner
WBMG, Inc.

Robert Lockwood
Principal
News Graphics

John MacFarlane
Editor
Financial Times of Canada

David Hillman
Partner
Pentagram Design UK

Claude Maggiore
Founder and Creative Director
Editorial

JOYCE RAVID

HERB LUBALIN AWARD (HENRY WOLF)

Henry Wolf views design as an act of translation. Visual imagery is as precise as the written word. In translating words into images, Henry Wolf has traveled on many divergent paths, but his design solutions appear simple, even as the work is subtle and complex.

His career began in 1946 in a two-man art studio, having arrived in 1941 from Vienna and then serving in the U.S. Army. In 1952, he started as a designer at *Esquire*, becoming art director in a few months, working with Arnold Gingrich, the founding editor. Becoming restless, he moved to *Harper's Bazaar* in 1958 as art director, where he had a tremendous reputation to uphold: his predecessor was Alexey Brodovitch. During his tenure, he changed the layout, the typography and the photographic contributors, but all subtly with his great sense of graphics, his eye for photography, and his genius for design. While working with Nancy White and Diana Vreeland, he acquired his good fashion sense. In 1961, he was presented the opportunity to start a new magazine for the performing arts called *Show*, which became the last opulent American magazine.

In 1956, he entered the advertising world, signing on as art director with McCann Erickson, working with its chairman Paul Foley whose approach taught Henry the value of humor, modesty and style. Here, Henry was involved in creating campaigns for Alka-Seltzer, Buick, Aqueduct Race Track, Coca-Cola, Philip Morris and other accounts.

In 1972, Henry opened his own firm with Doris Shaw, advertising director of Saks Fifth Avenue. He was instrumental in developing the catalog-as-magazine. A great variety of advertising assignments came his way as he expanded into television and film for such clients as Revlon and IBM. Henry has always kept his hand in magazines including designs and redesigns for *Business Week, House Beautiful, Sesame Street, ABC Cable*, and the original *Dial* for PBS; house organs for B.F. Goodrich, RCA, Champion International; and covers for *Time, New York, Holiday, Money* and many others.

His profession has bestowed upon him many of its highest distinctions. He was inducted into the Art Directors Club Hall of Fame in 1980, received the Gold Medal of the AIGA in 1976, and, in 1970, was made a Benjamin Franklin Fellow of the Royal Society of Arts and Sciences. He is also a board member of the International Design Conference in Aspen. He has taught new generations at Cooper Union, School of Visual Arts, and continues to teach at Parsons School of Design.

His most recent work is a new book entitled "Visual Thinking: Methods for making images memorable," which was published in November 1988 by American Showcase.

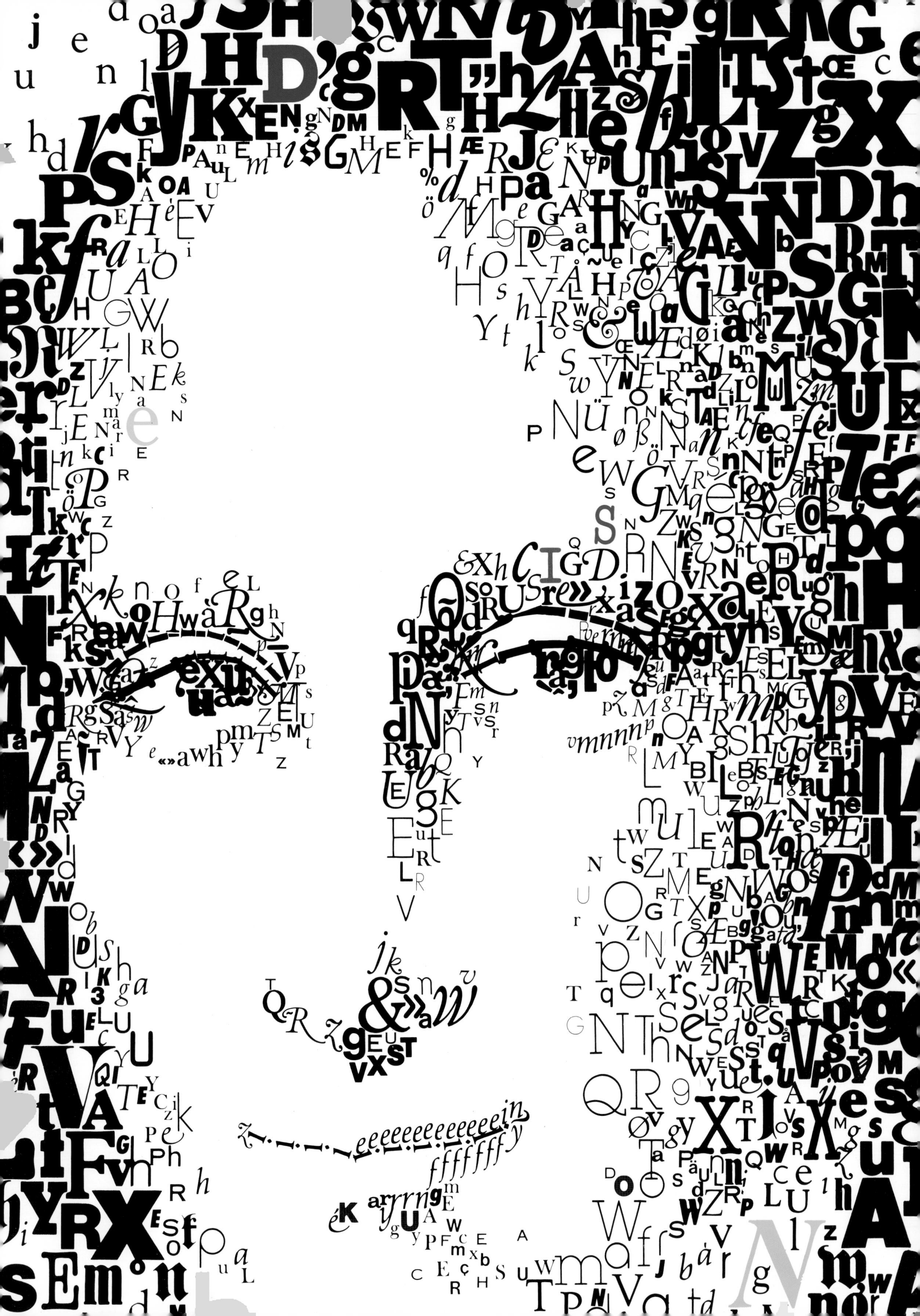

PUBLICATION **Spy**
ART DIRECTOR **Alex Isley**
DESIGNER **Cathy Gilmore-Barnes**
PUBLISHER **Spy Publishing Partners**
CATEGORY **Single Page/Spread**
DATE **May 1988**

Gold

PUBLICATION **Italian Vogue**
ART DIRECTOR **Fabien Baron**
PUBLISHER **Condé Nast International Inc.**
CATEGORY **Single Page/Spread**

PUBLICATION **Italian Vogue**
ART DIRECTOR **Fabien Baron**
ILLUSTRATOR **Georgia O'Keefe**
PUBLISHER **Condé Nast International, Inc.**
CATEGORY **Single Page/Spread**
DATE **December 1988**

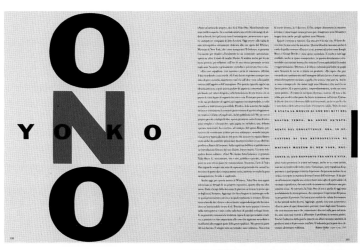

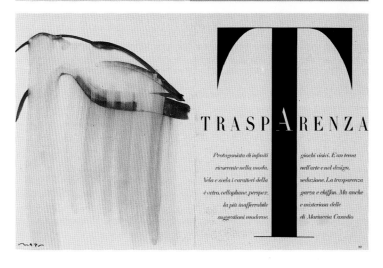

PUBLICATION **Italian Vogue**
ART DIRECTOR **Fabien Baron**
PHOTOGRAPHER **Satochi**
PUBLISHER **Condé Nast International, Inc.**
CATEGORY **Cover**
DATE **September 1988**

PUBLICATION **Italian Vogue**
ART DIRECTOR **Fabien Baron**
ILLUSTRATOR **Matts, Gustavsonn**
PUBLISHER **Condé Nast International, Inc.**
CATEGORY **Single Page/Spread**
DATE **November 1988**

PUBLICATION **Goucher College Annual Report**
ART DIRECTOR **Kate Berquist, Anthony Rutka**
DESIGNER **Kate Berquist**
ILLUSTRATOR **Gary Kelley**
PHOTOGRAPHER **Barry Holniker**
CLIENT **Goucher College**
AGENCY **Rutka/Weadock Design, Baltimore, MD**
CATEGORY **Single Issue**
DATE **December 1988**

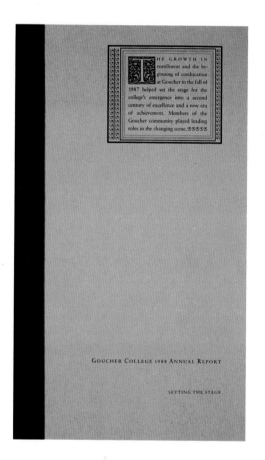

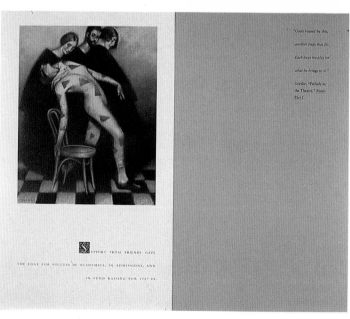

Gold

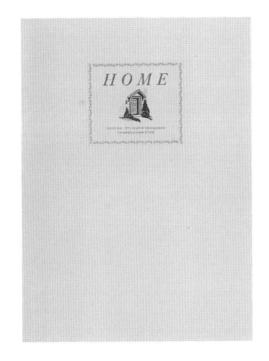

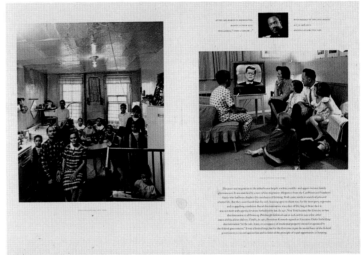

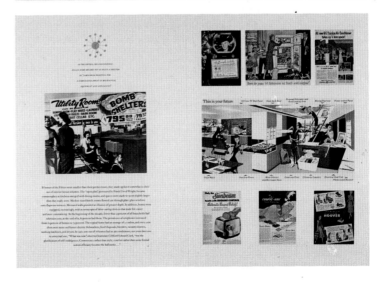

PUBLICATION **Fannie Mae-Home Annual Report**
ART DIRECTOR **Peter Harrison, Susan Hochbaum**
DESIGNER **Susan Hochbaum**
PHOTO EDITOR **Diane Cook**
CLIENT **Fannie Mae**
AGENCY **Pentagram Design, NYC**
CATEGORY **Single Issue**
DATE **April 1988**

PUBLICATION **Italian Vogue**
ART DIRECTOR **Fabien Baron**
DESIGNER **Felice Perini**
PHOTOGRAPHER **Guido Moccafico**
PUBLISHER **Condé Nast International, Inc.**
CATEGORY **Single Page/Spread**

PUBLICATION **Italian Vogue**
ART DIRECTOR **Fabien Baron**
PHOTOGRAPHER **Peter Lindbergh**
PUBLISHER **Condé Nast International Inc.**
CATEGORY **Single Page/Spread**

14

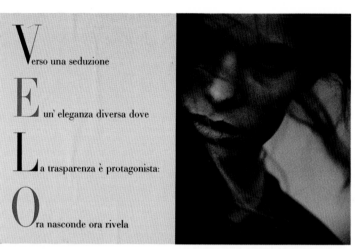

PUBLICATION **Italian Vogue**
ART DIRECTOR **Fabien Baron**
PHOTOGRAPHER **Arthur Elgort**
PUBLISHER **Condé Nast International, Inc.**
CATEGORY **Single Page/Spread**
DATE **December 1988**

PUBLICATION **Italian Vogue**
ART DIRECTOR **Fabien Baron**
PUBLISHER **Condé Nast International, Inc.**
CATEGORY **Single Page/Spread**

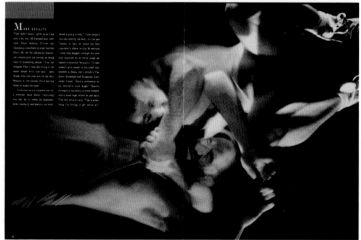

PUBLICATION **Life**
ART DIRECTOR **Tom Bentkowski**
DESIGNER **Nora Sheehan**
PHOTOGRAPHER **Gregory Heisler**
PUBLISHER **Time, Inc.**
CATEGORY **Story Presentation**
DATE **October 1988**

PUBLICATION **Arena**
ART DIRECTOR **Neville Brody**
DESIGNER **Neville Brody**
CATEGORY **Single Issue**

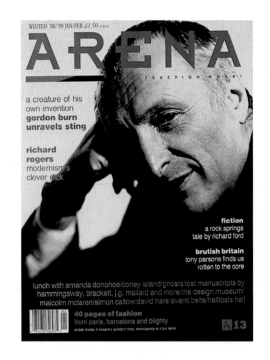

16

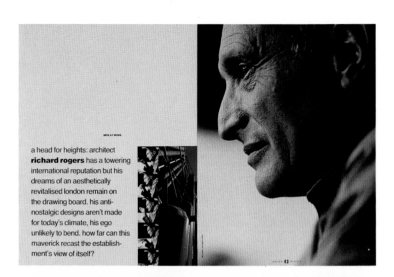

a head for heights: architect **richard rogers** has a towering international reputation but his dreams of an aesthetically revitalised london remain on the drawing board. his anti-nostalgic designs aren't made for today's climate, his ego unlikely to bend. how far can this maverick recast the establishment's view of itself?

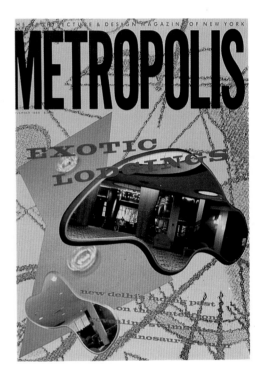

PUBLICATION **Metropolis**
ART DIRECTOR **Helene Silverman**
DESIGNER **Helene Silverman, Jeff Christensen**
PUBLISHER **Bellerophon Publications**
CATEGORY **Single Issue**
DATE **November 1988**

PUBLICATION **Wigwag**
ART DIRECTOR **Paul Davis**
DESIGNER **Paul Davis, Jose Condé , Jeanine Esposito**
PUBLISHER **Wigwag**
CATEGORY **New Magazine**
DATE **Summer 1988**

18

Silver

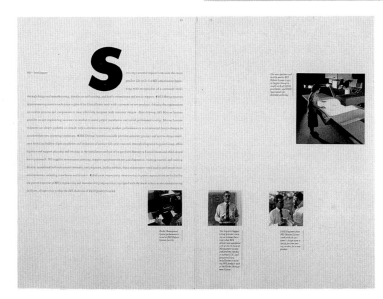

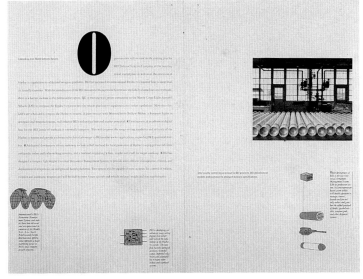

PUBLICATION **BEI Electronics Annual Report**
ART DIRECTOR **Steven Tolleson**
DESIGNER **Steven Tolleson, Nancy Paynter**
ILLUSTRATOR **Nancy Paynter**
PHOTOGRAPHER **Steven Unze**
CLIENT **BEI Electronics, Inc.**
AGENCY **Tolleson Design, San Francisco, CA**
CATEGORY **Single Issue**
DATE **January 1988**

PUBLICATION **Chili's, Inc. Annual Report**
ART DIRECTOR **Brian Boyd**
DESIGNER **Brian Boyd**
ILLUSTRATOR **Regan Dunnick**
PHOTOGRAPHER **Robert LaTorre**
CLIENT **Chili's, Inc.**
AGENCY **The Richards Group, Dallas, TX**
CATEGORY **Single Issue**
DATE **September 1988**

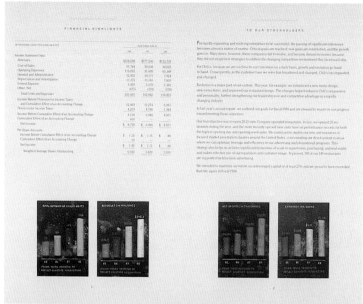

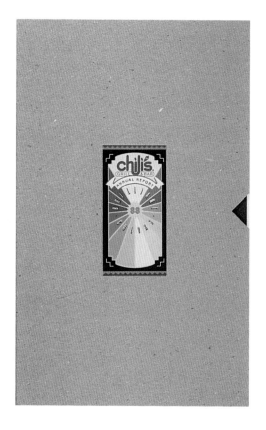

Silver

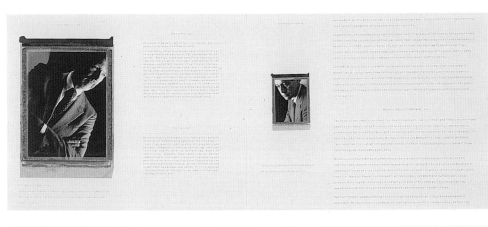

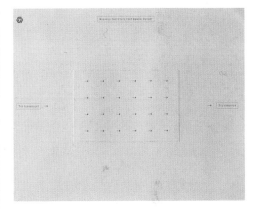

PUBLICATION **Nichols Institute Annual Report**
ART DIRECTOR **Jim Berte**
DESIGNER **Jim Berte**
PHOTOGRAPHER **Scott Morgan**
CLIENT **Nichols Institute**
AGENCY **Robert Miles Runyan & Associates, Playa del Rey, CA**
CATEGORY **Single Issue**
DATE **March 1988**

PUBLICATION **Zoo Views**
ART DIRECTOR **Ken Cook**
DESIGNER **Ken Cook**
PHOTOGRAPHER **Steven Underwood, John Blaustein**
PUBLISHER **San Francisco Zoo**
CATEGORY **Single Issue**

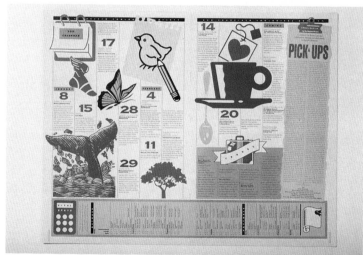

Silver

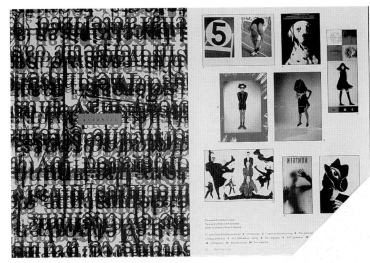

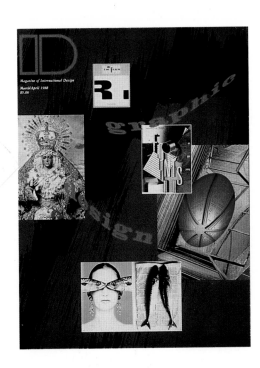

PUBLICATION **ID**
ART DIRECTOR **Gregory Mastrianni**
DESIGNERS **M & Co., Michael Bierut,
Katherine McCoy, David Frej, Marshall Arisman,
Tom Bonauro, Cheryl Heller, Helene Silverman,
Chris Callis, Rudy Vanderlans, Zuzana Licko**
PUBLISHER **Design Publications, Inc.**
CATEGORY **Single Issue**
DATE **March/April 1988**

PUBLICATION **Critical Issues**
DESIGN DIRECTOR **Barry Deck**
ART DIRECTOR **Kym Abrams**
DESIGNER **Barry Deck**
ILLUSTRATOR **Mary Flock**
PHOTOGRAPHER **Eric Hausman**
CLIENT **Lutheran General Hospital**
AGENCY **Kym Abrams Design, NYC**
CATEGORY **New Magazine**
DATE **Second Quarter 1988**

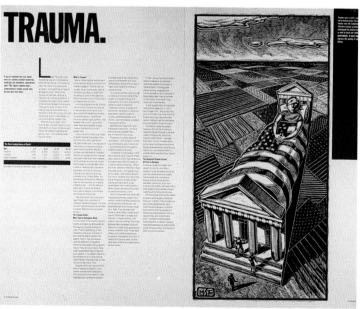

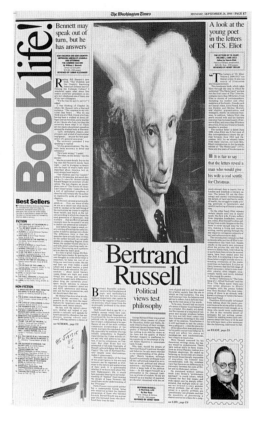

PUBLICATION **Washington Times**
DESIGN DIRECTOR **Joseph Scopin**
ART DIRECTOR **John Kascht**
DESIGNER **John Kascht**
ILLUSTRATOR **John Kascht**
PUBLISHER **The Washington Times**
CATEGORY **Cover**
DATE **September 26, 1988**

PUBLICATION **Details**
ART DIRECTOR **Lesley Vinson**
DESIGNER **Lesley Vinson**
PHOTOGRAPHER **John Chan**
PUBLISHER **Advance Publishing Corporation**
CATEGORY **Cover**
DATE **August 1988**

PUBLICATION **Italian Vogue**
ART DIRECTOR **Fabien Baron**
PHOTOGRAPHER **Steven Meisel**
PUBLISHER **Condé Nast International, Inc.**
CATEGORY **Cover**
DATE **November 1988**

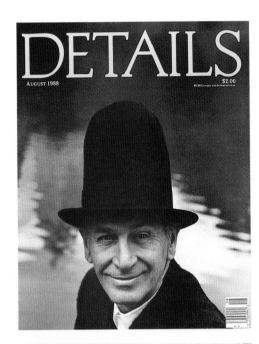

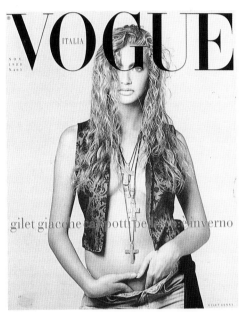

PUBLICATION **Details**
ART DIRECTOR **Lesley Vinson**
DESIGNER **Lesley Vinson**
PHOTOGRAPHER **Stephane Sednaoui**
PUBLISHER **Advance Publishing Corporation**
CATEGORY **Cover**
DATE **June 1988**

PUBLICATION **Italian Vogue**
ART DIRECTOR **Fabien Baron**
PUBLISHER **Condé Nast International, Inc.**
CATEGORY **Cover**
DATE **December 1988**

PUBLICATION **New York**
ART DIRECTOR **Robert Best**
PUBLISHER **News Group America**
CATEGORY **Cover**
DATE **April 4, 1988**

PUBLICATION **San Francisco Focus**
ART DIRECTOR **Matthew Drace**
DESIGNER **Matthew Drace**
PHOTOGRAPHER **David Peterson**
PUBLISHER **KQED, Inc.**
CATEGORY **Cover**
DATE **February 1988**

PUBLICATION **The Boston Globe Magazine**
ART DIRECTOR **Lucy Bartholomay**
DESIGNER **Lucy Bartholomay**
ILLUSTRATOR **Anita Kunz**
PUBLISHER **The Boston Globe**
CATEGORY **Cover**
DATE **January 24, 1988**

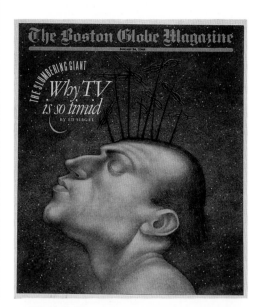

26

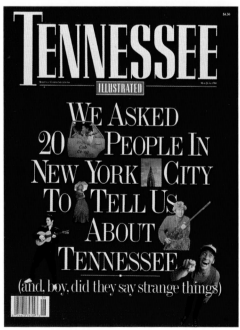

PUBLICATION **Tennessee Illustrated**
ART DIRECTOR **Mary Workman**
DESIGNER **Mary Workman**
PUBLISHER **Whittle Communications**
CATEGORY **Cover**
DATE **May/June 1988**

PUBLICATION **San Francisco Focus**
ART DIRECTOR **Matthew Drace**
DESIGNER **Matthew Drace**
PHOTOGRAPHER **Geof Kern**
PUBLISHER **KQED, Inc.**
CATEGORY **Cover**
DATE **June 1988**

PUBLICATION **Dallas Life Magazine**
ART DIRECTOR **Lesley Becker**
DESIGNER **Lesley Becker**
PHOTOGRAPHER **Brian Barnaud**
PUBLISHER **Dallas Morning News**
CATEGORY **Cover**
DATE **July 24, 1988**

PUBLICATION **Time**
ART DIRECTOR **Rudolph Hoglund**
DESIGNER **Tom Bentkowski**
PUBLISHER **Time, Inc.**
CATEGORY **Cover**
DATE **August 15, 1988**

PUBLICATION **National Geographic**
ART DIRECTOR **Howard E. Paine**
DESIGNER **Gerard A. Valerio**
PHOTOGRAPHER **Bruce Dale**
PUBLISHER **National Geographic Society**
CATEGORY **Cover**
DATE **December 1988**

PUBLICATION **Spy**
ART DIRECTOR **B.W. Honeycutt**
PHOTOGRAPHER **Douglas Kirkland, Sygma,**
Nolla Tully, Rick Friedman, Black Star
PUBLISHER **Spy Publishing Partners**
CATEGORY **Cover**
DATE **October 1988**

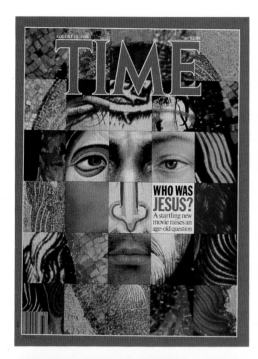

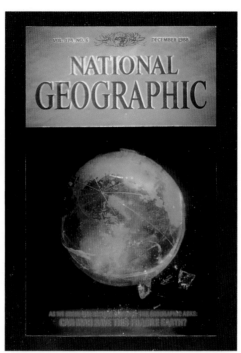

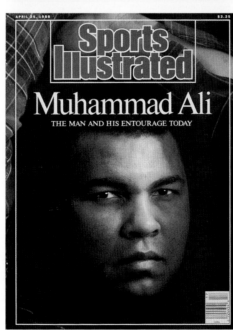

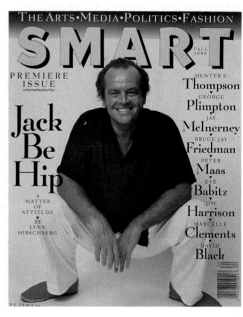

PUBLICATION **Time**
ART DIRECTOR **Rudolph Hoglund**
DESIGNER **Mirko Ilic**
PHOTOGRAPHER **Roberto Brosan**
PUBLISHER **Time, Inc.**
CATEGORY **Cover**
DATE **September 12, 1988**

PUBLICATION **Sports Illustrated**
ART DIRECTOR **Steven Hoffman**
DESIGNER **Steven Hoffman**
PHOTOGRAPHER **Gregory Heisler**
PUBLISHER **Time, Inc.**
CATEGORY **Cover**
DATE **April 25, 1988**

PUBLICATION **Smart**
ART DIRECTOR **Janet Waegel**
DESIGNER **Roger Black**
PHOTOGRAPHER **Michael O'Neil**
PUBLISHER **Smart American, Inc.**
CATEGORY **Cover**
DATE **Fall 1988**

PUBLICATION **Rolling Stone**
ART DIRECTOR **Fred Woodward**
DESIGNER **Fred Woodward**
PHOTOGRAPHER **Matt Mahurin**
PHOTO EDITOR **Laurie Kratochvil**
PUBLISHER **Straight Arrow Publishers**
CATEGORY **Cover**
DATE **February 11, 1988**

PUBLICATION **Rolling Stone**
ART DIRECTOR **Fred Woodward**
DESIGNER **Fred Woodward**
PHOTOGRAPHER **Bonnie Schiffman**
PHOTO EDITOR **Jim Franco**
PUBLISHER **Straight Arrow Publishers**
CATEGORY **Cover**
DATE **February 25, 1988**

PUBLICATION **Rolling Stone**
ART DIRECTOR **Fred Woodward**
DESIGNER **Fred Woodward**
ILLUSTRATOR **Paul Davis**
PUBLISHER **Straight Arrow Publishers**
CATEGORY **Cover**
DATE **April 7, 1988**

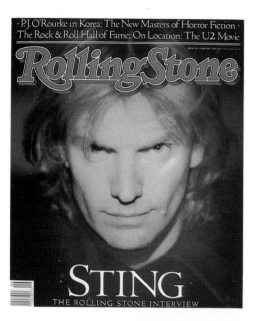

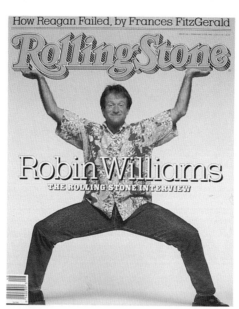

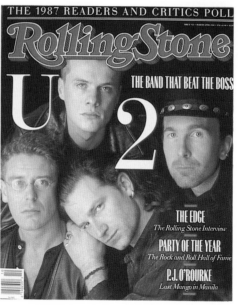

PUBLICATION **Rolling Stone**
ART DIRECTOR **Fred Woodward**
DESIGNER **Fred Woodward**
PHOTOGRAPHER **Matthew Rolston**
PHOTO EDITOR **Laurie Kratochvil**
PUBLISHER **Straight Arrow Publishers**
CATEGORY **Cover**
DATE **May 19, 1988**

PUBLICATION **Rolling Stone**
ART DIRECTOR **Fred Woodward**
DESIGNER **Fred Woodward**
PHOTOGRAPHER **Matthew Rolston**
PHOTO EDITOR **Laurie Kratochvil**
PUBLISHER **Straight Arrow Publishers**
CATEGORY **Cover**
DATE **March 10, 1988**

PUBLICATION **Maxwell House Messenger**
DESIGN DIRECTOR **Iris Brown**
ART DIRECTOR **Janice Fudyma**
PHOTOGRAPHER **Richard Levy, Tornberg/Coghlan**
CLIENT **Maxwell House**
AGENCY **Bernhardt/Fudyma Design Group, NYC**
CATEGORY **Cover**
DATE **September 1988**

PUBLICATION **Visions: BF/VF**
ART DIRECTOR **Marc English**
PHOTOGRAPHER **Shari Robertson,
David Feingold, Cecilia Condéit**
PHOTO EDITOR **Ann Marie Stein**
CLIENT **Boston Film/Video Foundation**
CATEGORY **Cover**
DATE **Summer 1988**

PUBLICATION **UNISYS Performance**
ART DIRECTOR **Eric Madsen**
DESIGNER **Eric Madsen, Tim Sauer**
PHOTOGRAPHER **Kerry Peterson**
PHOTO EDITOR **Gary Teagarden**
CLIENT **UNISYS Defense System**
AGENCY **Madsen & Kuenster, Minneapolis, MN**
CATEGORY **Cover**
DATE **Fall 1988**

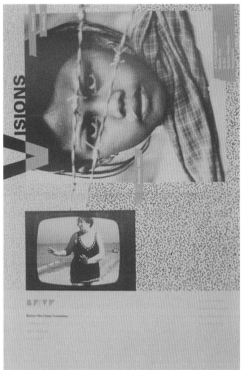

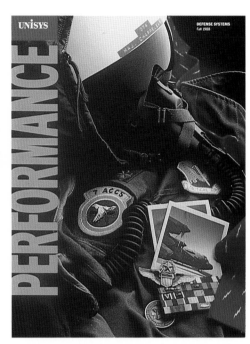

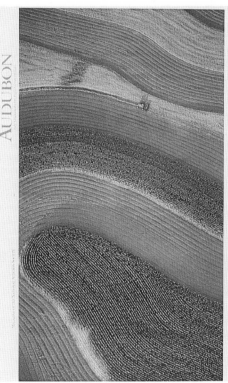

PUBLICATION **MMA Bulletin**
DESIGN DIRECTOR **Betty Binns**
ART DIRECTOR **Joan Holt**
DESIGNER **David Skolkin**
PUBLISHER **Metropolitan Museum Of Art**
CATEGORY **Cover**
DATE **Spring 1988**

PUBLICATION **Audubon**
ART DIRECTOR **D. J. McClain**
DESIGNER **D. J. McClain**
PHOTOGRAPHER **R. Hamilton Smith**
PUBLISHER **National Audobon Society**
CATEGORY **Cover**
DATE **July 1988**

PUBLICATION **Agenda**
DESIGN DIRECTOR **Eric Keller**
ART DIRECTOR **Sharon Marson**
ILLUSTRATOR **Cathy Gendron**
CLIENT **Chrysler Motor Company**
AGENCY **The Publications Co., Dallas, TX**
CATEGORY **Cover**
DATE **September 30, 1988**

PUBLICATION **Directions**
DESIGN DIRECTOR **Martin Gregg, Monique Davis**
ART DIRECTOR **Christina Weber**
PUBLISHER **The District Collaborative, Denver, CO**
CATEGORY **Cover**
DATE **December 1988**

PUBLICATION **Individual Banker**
DESIGN DIRECTOR **K. Mc David**
ART DIRECTOR **Tana Klugherz**
DESIGNER **Tana Klugherz**
ILLUSTRATOR **Mark Hess**
CLIENT **Chase Manhattan**
AGENCY **Tana & Co., NYC**
CATEGORY **Cover**
DATE **December 1988**

PUBLICATION **Studio**
ART DIRECTOR **Alfredo Muccino**
DESIGNER **Alfredo Muccino**
CLIENT **Western Art Directors Club**
AGENCY **Muccino Design Group, San Jose, CA**
CATEGORY **Cover**
DATE **June 1988**

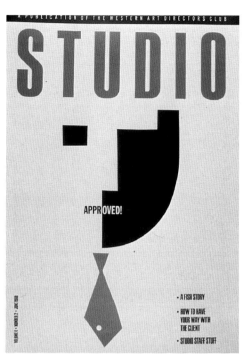

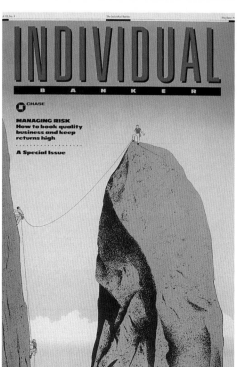

PUBLICATION **Directions**
DESIGN DIRECTOR **Monique Davis**
ART DIRECTOR **Christina Weber**
PUBLISHER **The District Collaborative, Denver, CO**
CATEGORY **Cover**
DATE **Winter 1988**

PUBLICATION **Individual Banker**
DESIGN DIRECTOR **K. Mc David**
ART DIRECTOR **Tana Klugherz**
DESIGNER **Tana Klugherz**
ILLUSTRATOR **Guy Billout**
CLIENT **Chase Manhattan Bank**
AGENCY **Tana & Co., NYC**
CATEGORY **Cover**
DATE **June 1988**

PUBLICATION **Studio**
ART DIRECTOR **Alfredo Muccino**
DESIGNER **Alfredo Muccino**
CLIENT **Western Art Directors Club**
AGENCY **Muccino Design Group, San Jose, CA**
CATEGORY **Cover**
DATE **Fall 1988**

PUBLICATION **Adweek Special Report**
ART DIRECTOR **Carole Erger-Fass**
DESIGNER **Elizabeth Chinman**
ILLUSTRATOR **Richard McNeel**
Adweek

PUBLICATION **Product Marketing**
DESIGN DIRECTOR **Marjorie Crane**
ART DIRECTOR **Victoria Green**
PHOTOGRAPHER **Susan Goldman**
PUBLISHER **International Thomson Retail Press**
CATEGORY **Cover**
DATE **February 1988**

PUBLICATION **The Clarion**
ART DIRECTOR **Faye Eng, Anthony Yee**
DESIGNER **Faye Eng, Anthony Yee**
PHOTOGRAPHER **Frank Maresca, Edward Shoffstall**
PUBLISHER **Museum of American Folk Art**
CATEGORY **Cover**
DATE **Fall 1988**

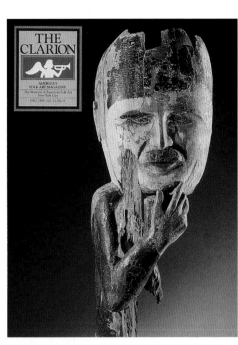

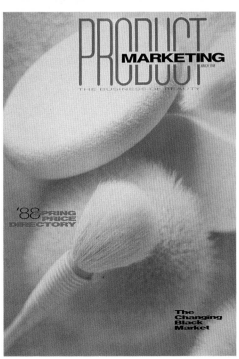

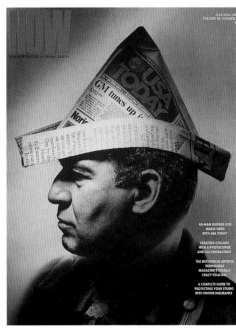

PUBLICATION **Mobile Communications**
ART DIRECTOR **Glenn Mosser**
DESIGNER **Rachael Gerst**
ILLUSTRATOR **Rachael Gerst**
PUBLISHER **Phillips Publishing**
CATEGORY **Cover**
DATE **August 1988**

PUBLICATION **Product Marketing**
DESIGN DIRECTOR **Marjorie Crane**
ART DIRECTOR **Victoria Green**
PHOTOGRAPHER **Gary Buss**
PUBLISHER **International Thomson Retail Press**
CATEGORY **Cover**
DATE **March 1988**

PUBLICATION **How**
ART DIRECTOR **Scott Menchin**
DESIGNER **Scott Menchin**
PHOTOGRAPHER **William Duke**
PUBLISHER **F & W Publishing**
CATEGORY **Cover**
DATE **July/August 1988**

PUBLICATION **Architectural Record**
DESIGN DIRECTOR **Alberto Bucchianeri**
DESIGNER **Anna-Egger Schlesinger**
PHOTOGRAPHER **Steve Rosenthal**
PUBLISHER **McGraw-Hill**
CATEGORY **Cover**
DATE **March 1988**

PUBLICATION **Architectural Record**
DESIGN DIRECTOR **Alberto Bucchianeri**
DESIGNER **Anna-Egger Schlesinger**
PHOTOGRAPHER **PetrAaron, Esto**
PUBLISHER **McGraw-Hill**
CATEGORY **Cover**
DATE **April 1988**

PUBLICATION **Architectural Record**
DESIGN DIRECTOR **Alberto Bucchianeri**
DESIGNER **Alberto Bucchianeri**
PHOTOGRAPHER **Paul Warchol**
PUBLISHER **McGraw-Hill**
CATEGORY **Cover**
DATE **February 1988**

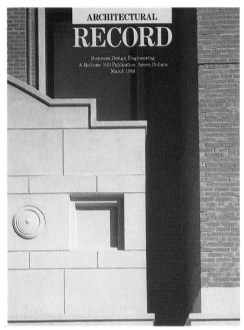
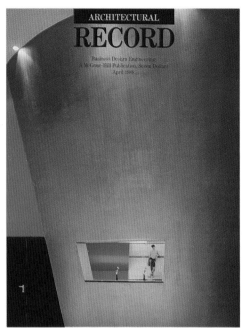
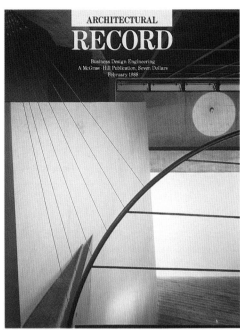

PUBLICATION **Graphis**
ART DIRECTOR **B. Martin Pedersen**
DESIGNER **B. Martin Pedersen**
PHOTOGRAPHER **Manfred Rieker Studio**
PUBLISHER **Graphis Publishing Corporation**
CATEGORY **Cover**
DATE **October 1988**

PUBLICATION **Graphis**
ART DIRECTOR **B. Martin Pedersen**
DESIGNER **B. Martin Pedersen**
PUBLISHER **Graphis Publishing Corporation**
CATEGORY **Cover**
DATE **December 1988**

PUBLICATION **Graphis**
ART DIRECTOR **B. Martin Pedersen**
DESIGNER **B. Martin Pedersen**
PUBLISHER **Graphis Publishing Corporation**
CATEGORY **Cover**
DATE **April 1988**

PUBLICATION **Progressive Architecture**
ART DIRECTOR **Richelle Huff**
DESIGNER **Richelle Huff**
PHOTOGRAPHER **Gabriele Basilico**
PUBLISHER **Penton Publishing**
CATEGORY **Cover**
DATE **September 1988**

PUBLICATION **Progressive Architecture**
ART DIRECTOR **Richelle Huff**
DESIGNER **Lisa M. Mangano**
PHOTOGRAPHER **Steven Brooke**
PUBLISHER **Penton Publishing**
CATEGORY **Cover**
DATE **December 1988**

PUBLICATION **Art Direction**
DESIGNER **Bonnie Segal**
ILLUSTRATOR **Bonnie Segal**
PUBLISHER **Art Direction**
CATEGORY **Cover**
DATE **September 1988**

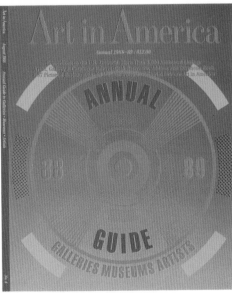

PUBLICATION **Progressive Architecture**
ART DIRECTOR **Richelle Huff**
DESIGNER **Richelle Huff**
PHOTOGRAPHER **Stephane Couturier**
PUBLISHER **Penton Publishing**
CATEGORY **Cover**
DATE **June 1988**

PUBLICATION **Progressive Architecture**
ART DIRECTOR **Richelle Huff**
DESIGNER **Richelle Huff**
PHOTOGRAPHER **Timothy Hursley**
PUBLISHER **Penton Publishing**
CATEGORY **Cover**
DATE **February 1988**

PUBLICATION **Art in America**
ART DIRECTOR **Kate Wodell**
DESIGNER **David Curry**
PUBLISHER **Brant Publications**
CATEGORY **Cover**
DATE **August 1988**

PUBLICATION **Industrial Launderer**
ART DIRECTOR **Jack Lefkowitz**
DESIGNER **Jack Lefkowitz**
ILLUSTRATOR **M. V. Strnad**
PUBLISHER **Institute of Industrial Launderers**
CATEGORY **Cover**
DATE **February 1988**

PUBLICATION **Industrial Launderer**
ART DIRECTOR **Jack Lefkowitz**
DESIGNER **Jack Lefkowitz**
ILLUSTRATOR **M. V. Strnad**
PUBLISHER **Institute of Industrial Launderers**
CATEGORY **Cover**
DATE **July 1988**

PUBLICATION **Industrial Launderer**
ART DIRECTOR **Jack Lefkowitz**
DESIGNER **Jack Lefkowitz**
ILLUSTRATOR **M. V. Strnad**
PUBLISHER **Institute of Industrial Launderers**
CATEGORY **Cover**
DATE **August 1988**

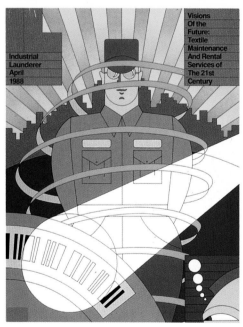

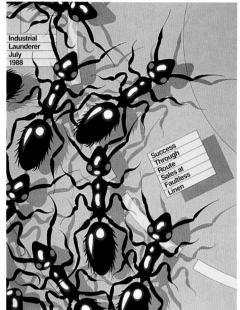

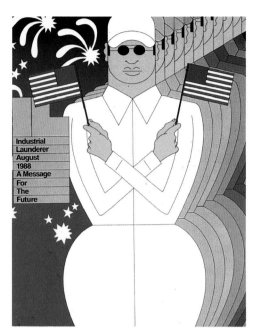

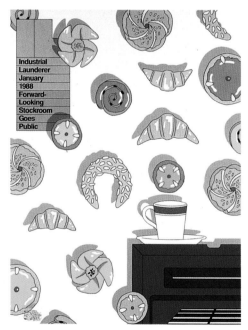

PUBLICATION **Industrial Launderer**
ART DIRECTOR **Jack Lefkowitz**
DESIGNER **Jack Lefkowitz**
ILLUSTRATOR **M. V. Strnad**
PUBLISHER **Institute of Industrial Launderers**
CATEGORY **Cover**
DATE **April 1988**

PUBLICATION **Industrial Launderer**
ART DIRECTOR **Jack Lefkowitz**
DESIGNER **Jack Lefkowitz**
ILLUSTRATOR **M. V. Strnad**
PUBLISHER **Institute of Industrial Launderers**
CATEGORY **Cover**
DATE **January 1988**

PUBLICATION **Industrial Launderer**
ART DIRECTOR **Jack Lefkowitz**
DESIGNER **Jack Lefkowitz**
ILLUSTRATOR **M. V. Strnad**
PUBLISHER **Institute of Industrial Launderers**
CATEGORY **Cover**
DATE **March 1988**

PUBLICATION **Iron & Steelmaker**
ART DIRECTOR **Jeff Lunderstadt**
DESIGNER **Jeff Lunderstadt**
PUBLISHER **Iron & Steel Society**
CATEGORY **Cover**
DATE **July 1988**

PUBLICATION **Electronic Engineering Times**
ART DIRECTOR **Mira Ramji-Stein**
DESIGNER **Mira Ramji-Stein**
ILLUSTRATOR **Jonh Ellis**
PUBLISHER **CMP Publications, Inc.**
CATEGORY **Cover**
DATE **March 3, 1988**

PUBLICATION **Seven Days**
ART DIRECTOR **John Belknap**
DESIGNER **Jean-Claude Suares, John Belknap, Claudia Lebenthal**
ILLUSTRATOR **Marc Rosenthal, Les Kanturek, Christoph Hitz**
PHOTOGRAPHER **Adrian Boot, Retna Ltd.**
PUBLISHER **Stern Publishing**
CATEGORY **Cover**
DATE **May 4, 1988**

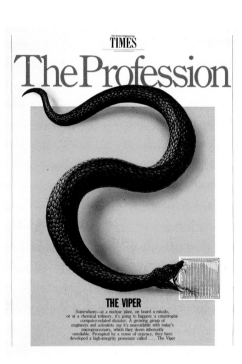

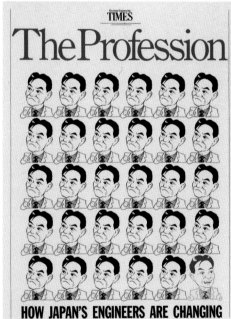

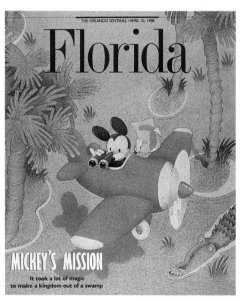

PUBLICATION **Electronic Engineering Times**
ART DIRECTOR **Mira Ramji-Stein**
DESIGNER **Mira Ramji-Stein**
ILLUSTRATOR **Seiji Matsumoto**
PUBLISHER **CMP Publications, Inc.**
CATEGORY **Cover**
DATE **December 5,1988**

PUBLICATION **Florida - The Orlando Sentinel**
ART DIRECTOR **Santa Choplin**
DESIGNER **Santa Choplin**
ILLUSTRATOR **John Ceballos**
PUBLISHER **The Orlando Sentinel**
CATEGORY **Cover**
DATE **April 10, 1988**

PUBLICATION **The Washington Times**
ART DIRECTOR **John Kascht**
DESIGNER **John Kascht**
PUBLISHER **The Washington Times**
CATEGORY **Cover**
DATE **February 8, 1988**

PUBLICATION **The Washington Times**
ART DIRECTOR **Alex Hunter**
DESIGNER **Joseph Scopin**
ILLUSTRATOR **Alex Hunter**
PUBLISHER **The Washington Times**
CATEGORY **Cover**
DATE **October 20, 1988**

PUBLICATION **The Washington Times**
ART DIRECTOR **John kascht**
DESIGNER **Joseph Scopin**
PUBLISHER **The Washington Times**
CATEGORY **Cover**
DATE **October 3, 1988**

PUBLICATION **Wall Street Journal Reports**
DESIGN DIRECTOR **Greg Leeds**
ART DIRECTOR **Joe Dizney**
DESIGNER **Joe Dizney**
ILLUSTRATOR **Cathie Bleck**
PUBLISHER **Dow Jones & Company, Inc.**
CATEGORY **Cover**
DATE **March 18, 1988**

PUBLICATION **Rolling Stone**
ART DIRECTOR **Fred Woodward**
DESIGNER **Fred Woodward**
PHOTOGRAPHER **Albert Watson**
PHOTO EDITOR **Laurie Kratochvil**
PUBLISHER **Straight Arrow Publishers**
CATEGORY **Single Page/Spread**
DATE **October 6, 1988**

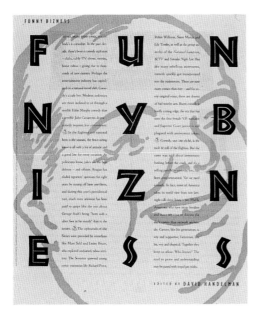

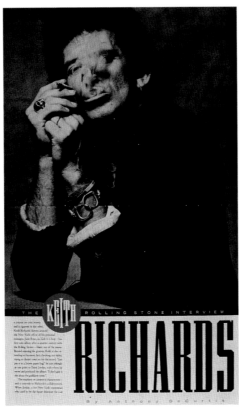

PUBLICATION **Rolling Stone**
ART DIRECTOR **Fred Woodward**
DESIGNER **Fred Woodward, Gail Anderson**
PUBLISHER **Straight Arrow Publishers**
CATEGORY **Single Page/Spread**
DATE **November 3, 1988**

PUBLICATION **Spy**
ART DIRECTOR **B.W. Honeycutt**
DESIGNER **Michael Hofmann**
ILLUSTRATOR **C.F. Payne**
PUBLISHER **Spy Publishing Partners**
CATEGORY **Single Page/Spread**
DATE **September 1988**

PUBLICATION **Rolling Stone**
ART DIRECTOR **Fred Woodward**
DESIGNER **Joel Cuyler**
PHOTOGRAPHER **Bonnie Schiffman**
PHOTO EDITOR **Jim Franco**
PUBLISHER **Straight Arrow Publishers**
CATEGORY **Single Page/Spread**
DATE **February 25,1988**

PUBLICATION **Rolling Stone**
ART DIRECTOR **Fred Woodward**
DESIGNER **Catherine Gilmore-Barnes**
PHOTOGRAPHER **Frank W. Ockenfels**
PHOTO EDITOR **Jim Franco**
PUBLISHER **Straight Arrow Publishers**
CATEGORY **Single Page/Spread**
DATE **June 30, 1988**

PUBLICATION **Rolling Stone**
ART DIRECTOR **Fred Woodward**
DESIGNER **Gail Anderson**
PHOTOGRAPHER **Herb Ritts**
PHOTO EDITOR **Laurie Kratochvil**
PUBLISHER **Straight Arrow Publishers**
CATEGORY **Single Page/Spread**
DATE **June 30, 1988**

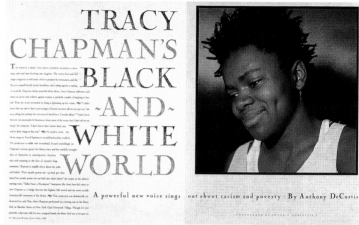

PUBLICATION **Rolling Stone**
ART DIRECTOR **Fred Woodward**
DESIGNER **Gail Anderson**
PHOTOGRAPHER **Brian Smale**
PHOTO EDITOR **Laurie Kratochvil**
PUBLISHER **Straight Arrow Publishers**
CATEGORY **Single Page/Spread**
DATE **December 1,1988**

PUBLICATION **Rolling Stone**
ART DIRECTOR **Fred Woodward**
DESIGNER **Joel Cuyler**
PHOTOGRAPHER **Hiro**
PHOTO EDITOR **Laurie Kratochvil**
PUBLISHER **Straight Arrow Publishers**
CATEGORY **Single Page/Spread**
DATE **April 21, 1988**

PUBLICATION **Rolling Stone**
ART DIRECTOR **Fred Woodward**
DESIGNER **Gail Anderson**
ILLUSTRATOR **Brian Cronin**
PUBLISHER **Straight Arrow Publishers**
CATEGORY **Single Page/Spread**
DATE **August 25, 1988**

PUBLICATION **Rolling Stone**
ART DIRECTOR **Fred Woodward**
DESIGNER **Fred Woodward**
ILLUSTRATOR **Matt Mahurin**
PUBLISHER **Straight Arrow Publishers**
CATEGORY **Single Page/Spread**
DATE **March 24, 1988**

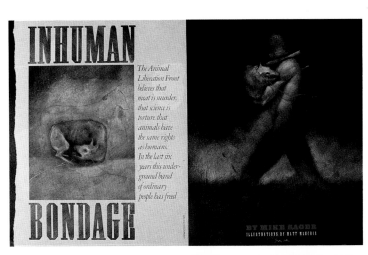

PUBLICATION **Rolling Stone**
ART DIRECTOR **Fred Woodward**
DESIGNER **Fred Woodward, Gail Anderson**
PHOTOGRAPHER **Matt Mahurin**
PHOTO EDITOR **Laurie Kratochvil**
PUBLISHER **Straight Arrow Publishers**
CATEGORY **Single Page/Spread**
DATE **October 6, 1988**

PUBLICATION **Rolling Stone**
ART DIRECTOR **Fred Woodward**
DESIGNER **Fred Woodward**
ILLUSTRATOR **Brian Cronin**
PUBLISHER **Straight Arrow Publishers**
CATEGORY **Single Page/Spread**
DATE **March 24, 1988**

PUBLICATION **Arena**
ART DIRECTOR **Neville Brody**
CATEGORY **Single Page/Spread**
DATE **Winter 1988**

PUBLICATION **Arena**
ART DIRECTOR **Neville Brody**
CATEGORY **Single Page/Spread**
DATE **Winter 1988**

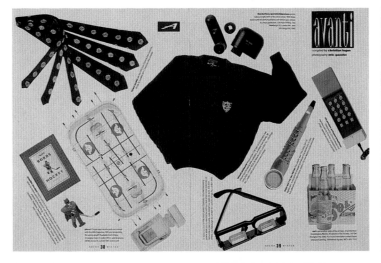

40

PUBLICATION **Arena**
ART DIRECTOR **Neville Brody**
CATEGORY **Single Page/Spread**
DATE **Winter 1988**

PUBLICATION **Arena**
ART DIRECTOR **Neville Brody**
CATEGORY **Single Page/Spread**
DATE **Winter 1988**

PUBLICATION **Spy**
ART DIRECTOR **B.W. Honeycutt**
DESIGNER **Scott Frommere**
PUBLISHER **Spy Publishing Partners**
CATEGORY **Single Page/Spread**
DATE **December 1988**

PUBLICATION **Spy**
ART DIRECTOR **Alexander Isley**
DESIGNER **Michael Hofmann**
PUBLISHER **Spy Publishing Partners**
CATEGORY **Single Page/Spread**
DATE **August 1988**

PUBLICATION **Spy**
ART DIRECTOR **Alexander Isley**
DESIGNER **Alexander Knowlton**
PUBLISHER **Spy Publishing Partners**
CATEGORY **Single Page/Spread**
DATE **March 1988**

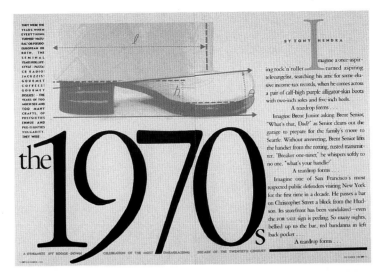

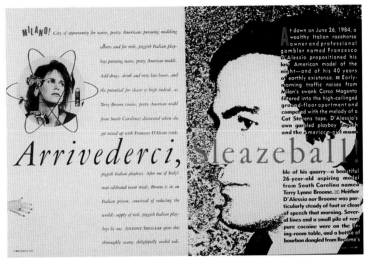

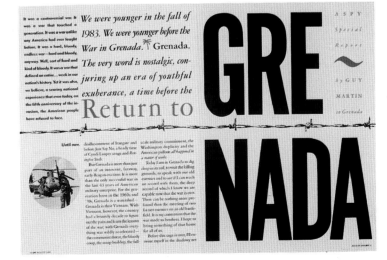

PUBLICATION **GQ**
ART DIRECTOR **Robert Priest**
DESIGNER **Mark Danzig**
ILLUSTRATOR **Matt Mahurin**
PUBLISHER **Condé Nast Publications, Inc.**
CATEGORY **Single Page/Spread**
DATE **August 1988**

PUBLICATION **GQ**
ART DIRECTOR **Robert Priest**
DESIGNER **Rhonda Rubenstein**
ILLUSTRATOR **Julian Allen**
PUBLISHER **Condé Nast Publications, Inc.**
CATEGORY **Single Page/Spread**
DATE **August 1988**

Tanya Gives Great *Glasnost*

At Moscow's Mezh Hotel, the caviar is cold and the women are hot. But be careful: Big Comradeski is watching

By MICHAEL WALSH

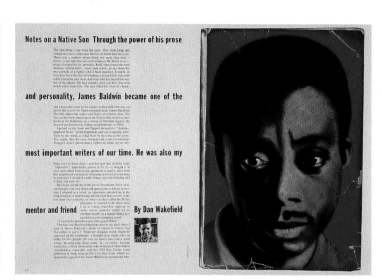

Notes on a Native Son Through the power of his prose

and personality, James Baldwin became one of the

most important writers of our time. He was also my

mentor and friend

By Dan Wakefield

sneak pitch

By John Lutz Photography by

Jacquet
Illinois

BY LARRY BIRNBAUM

Still Flying Home

PUBLICATION **Special Report/Fiction**
DESIGN DIRECTOR **Jim Darilek**
ART DIRECTOR **Alan Avery**
DESIGNER **Carol Williams**
PHOTOGRAPHER **Joseph Astor**
PUBLISHER **Whittle Communications**
CATEGORY **Single Page/Spread**
DATE **November 1988**

PUBLICATION **Musician**
ART DIRECTOR **David Carson**
DESIGNER **David Carson**
PHOTOGRAPHER **Enid Farber**
PUBLISHER **Billboard**
CATEGORY **Single Page/Spread**
DATE **December 1988**

PUBLICATION **Life**
ART DIRECTOR **Tom Bentkowski**
DESIGNER **Nora Sheehan**
PHOTOGRAPHER **Lee Crum**
PUBLISHER **Time, Inc.**
CATEGORY **Single Page/Spread**
DATE **May 1988**

PUBLICATION **Life**
ART DIRECTOR **Tom Bentkowski**
DESIGNER **Charles Pates**
PHOTOGRAPHER **Robert Cumins**
PUBLISHER **Time, Inc.**
CATEGORY **Single Page/Spread**
DATE **May 1988**

PUBLICATION **Sports Illustrated**
ART DIRECTOR **Steven Hoffman**
DESIGNER **Peter Herbert, Steven Hoffman**
PHOTOGRAPHER **Gregory Heisler**
PUBLISHER **Time, Inc.**
CATEGORY **Single Page/Spread**
DATE **April 15, 1988**

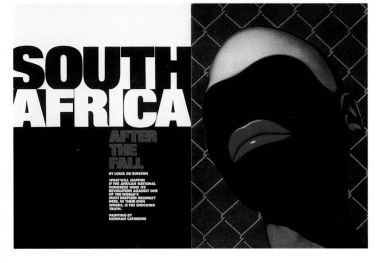

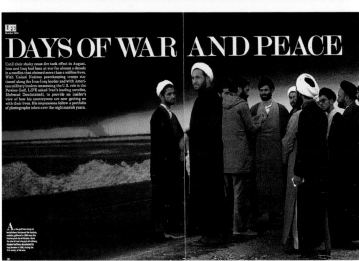

43

PUBLICATION **Life**
ART DIRECTOR **Tom Bentkowski**
DESIGNER **Robin E. Brown**
PHOTOGRAPHER **Manoocher, Sipa Press**
PUBLISHER **Time, Inc.**
CATEGORY **Single Page/Spread**
DATE **October 1988**

PUBLICATION **Penthouse**
DESIGN DIRECTOR **Frank Devino**
ART DIRECTOR **Richard Bleiweiss**
DESIGNER **Joseph Morello**
ILLUSTRATOR **Norman Catherine**
PUBLISHER **Penthouse International, Ltd.**
CATEGORY **Single Page/Spread**
DATE **March 1988**

PUBLICATION **Regardies**
ART DIRECTOR **John Korpics**
DESIGNER **John Korpics**
ILLUSTRATOR **Alan E. Cober**
PUBLISHER **Regardies, Inc.**
CATEGORY **Single Page/Spread**
DATE **October 1988**

PUBLICATION **PC World**
ART DIRECTOR **David Armario**
DESIGNER **David Armario**
ILLUSTRATOR **Brian Cronin**
PUBLISHER **PCW Communications**
CATEGORY **Single Page/Spread**
DATE **January 1988**

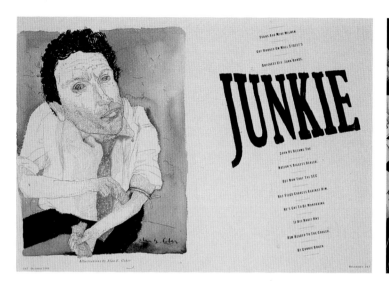

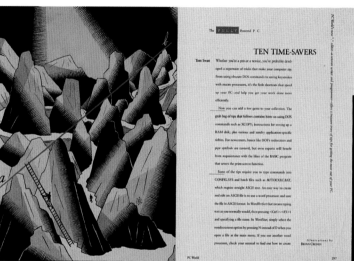

PUBLICATION **Savvy**
ART DIRECTOR **Gina Davis**
DESIGNER **John Lee**
ILLUSTRATOR **Janet Wooley**
PUBLISHER **Family Media, Inc.**
CATEGORY **Single Page/Spread**
DATE **October 1988**

PUBLICATION **Sports Illustrated**
ART DIRECTOR **Steven Hoffman**
DESIGNER **Darrin Perry, Steven Hoffman**
ILLUSTRATOR **Anita Kunz**
PUBLISHER **Time, Inc.**
CATEGORY **Single Page/Spread**
DATE **December 19, 1988**

PUBLICATION **GQ**
ART DIRECTOR **Robert Priest**
DESIGNER **Alejandro Gonzalez**
PHOTOGRAPHER **Richard Avedon**
PUBLISHER **Condé Nast Publications, Inc.**
CATEGORY **Single Page/Spread**
DATE **November 1988**

PUBLICATION **GQ**
ART DIRECTOR **Robert Priest**
DESIGNER **Alejandro Gonzalez**
PHOTOGRAPHER **Richard Avedon**
PUBLISHER **Condé Nast Publications, Inc.**
CATEGORY **Single Page/Spread**
DATE **September 1988**

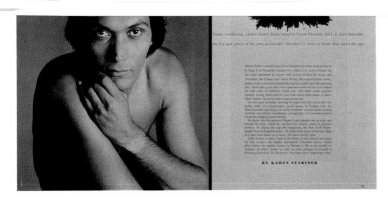

PUBLICATION **Regardies**
ART DIRECTOR **John Korpics**
DESIGNER **John Korpics**
PHOTOGRAPHER **Neil Selkirk**
PUBLISHER **Regardies, Inc.**
CATEGORY **Single Page/Spread**
DATE **October 1988**

PUBLICATION **GQ**
ART DIRECTOR **Robert Priest**
DESIGNER **Alejandro Gonzalez**
PHOTOGRAPHER **Chris Callis**
PUBLISHER **Condé Nast Publications, Inc.**
CATEGORY **Single Page/Spread**
DATE **August 1988**

PUBLICATION **Avenue**
DESIGN DIRECTOR **Carl S. Barile**
ART DIRECTOR **Mindy Ball**
ILLUSTRATOR **John Howard**
CATEGORY **Single Page/Spread**
DATE **November 1988**

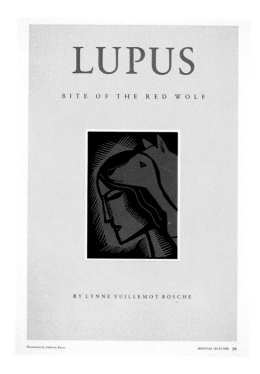

PUBLICATION **Medical Self Care**
ART DIRECTOR **Gordon Smith**
DESIGNER **Gordon Smith**
ILLUSTRATOR **Anthony Russo**
PUBLISHER **Medical Self Care, Inc.**
CATEGORY **Single Page/Spread**
DATE **March/April 1988**

PUBLICATION **Southern Style**
DESIGN DIRECTOR **Ken Smith**
ART DIRECTOR **Russell Noe**
DESIGNER **Russell Noe**
PHOTOGRAPHER **David Stewart**
PUBLISHER **Whittle Communications**
CATEGORY **Single Page/Spread**
DATE **November/December 1988**

PUBLICATION **The Boston Globe Magazine**
ART DIRECTOR **Lucy Bartholomay**
DESIGNER **Lucy Bartholomay**
PHOTOGRAPHER **Keith Jenkins**
PUBLISHER **The Boston Globe**
CATEGORY **Single Page/Spread**
DATE **June 19, 1988**

PUBLICATION **The Boston Globe Magazine**
ART DIRECTOR **Lucy Bartholomay**
DESIGNER **Lucy Bartholomay**
PUBLISHER **The Boston Globe**
CATEGORY **Single Page/Spread**
DATE **October 16, 1988**

PUBLICATION **The Boston Globe Magazine**
ART DIRECTOR **Lucy Bartholomay**
DESIGNER **Lucy Bartholomay**
PHOTOGRAPHER **Michele Clement**
PUBLISHER **The Boston Globe**
CATEGORY **Single Page/Spread**
DATE **October 2, 1988**

EUGENE O'NEILL LIVED HERE

BY SYLVIANE GOLD

KRONOS QUARTET

BY FRED KAPLAN

PUBLICATION **Musician**
ART DIRECTOR **David Carson**
DESIGNER **David Carson**
PHOTOGRAPHER **Russel Young**
PUBLISHER **Billboard**
CATEGORY **Single Page/Spread**
DATE **July 1988**

PUBLICATION **Detroit Monthly**
ART DIRECTOR **Michael Ban**
DESIGNER **Michael Ban**
PHOTOGRAPHER **Michelle Andonian**
PHOTO EDITOR **Michelle Andonian**
PUBLISHER **Crain Communications**
CATEGORY **Single Page/Spread**
DATE **March 1988**

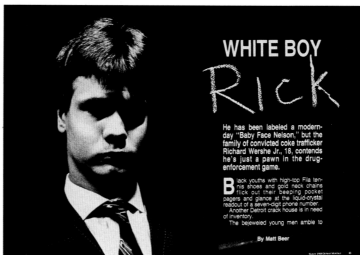

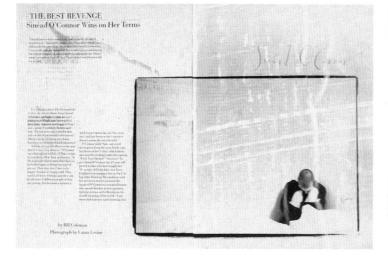

PUBLICATION **Musician**
ART DIRECTOR **David Carson**
DESIGNER **David Carson**
PHOTOGRAPHER **Laura Levine**
PUBLISHER **Billboard**
CATEGORY **Single Page/Spread**
DATE **June 1988**

PUBLICATION **The Boston Globe Magazine**
ART DIRECTOR **Lucy Bartholomay**
DESIGNER **Lucy Bartholomay**
PHOTOGRAPHER **Keith Jenkins**
PUBLISHER **The Boston Globe**
CATEGORY **Single Page/Spread**
DATE **August 28, 1988**

PUBLICATION **Premiere**
DESIGN DIRECTOR **Robert Best**
ART DIRECTOR **David Walters**
DESIGNER **Robert Best, MaryAnn Salvato, David Walters**
ILLUSTRATOR **Gary Halgren**
PHOTOGRAPHER **Alex Webb**
PUBLISHER **Murdoch**
CATEGORY **Single Page/Spread**
DATE **March 1988**

PUBLICATION **V**
DESIGN DIRECTOR **Terry R. Koppel**
ART DIRECTOR **Terry R. Koppel**
DESIGNER **Terry R. Koppel**
ILLUSTRATOR **Terry Allen**
PUBLISHER **Fairfield Publications**
CATEGORY **Single Page/Spread**
DATE **April 1988**

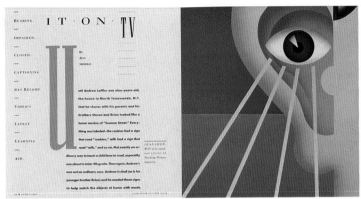

PUBLICATION **Premiere**
DESIGN DIRECTOR **Robert Best**
ART DIRECTOR **David Walters**
DESIGNER **Robert Best, David Walters, MaryAnn Salvato**
PHOTOGRAPHER **Susan Meiselas**
PUBLISHER **Murdoch**
CATEGORY **Single Page/Spread**
DATE **December 1988**

PUBLICATION **V**
DESIGN DIRECTOR **Terry R. Koppel**
ART DIRECTOR **Terry R. Koppel**
DESIGNER **Terry R. Koppel**
ILLUSTRATOR **Alexa Grace**
PUBLISHER **Fairfield Publications**
CATEGORY **Single Page/Spread**
DATE **April 1988**

PUBLICATION **Italian Vogue**
ART DIRECTOR **Fabien Baron**
PUBLISHER **Condé Nast International, Inc.**
CATEGORY **Single Page/Spread**
DATE **February 1988**

PUBLICATION **Italian Vogue**
ART DIRECTOR **Fabien Baron**
PUBLISHER **Condé Nast International, Inc.**
CATEGORY **Single Page/Spread**
DATE **February 1988**

PUBLICATION **Italian Vogue**
ART DIRECTOR **Fabien Baron**
PUBLISHER **Condé Nast International, Inc.**
CATEGORY **Single Page/Spread**
DATE **February 1988**

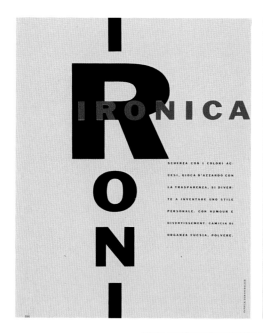

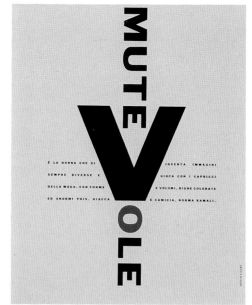

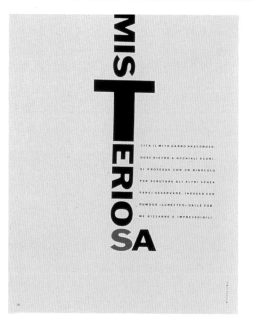

PUBLICATION **Italian Vogue**
ART DIRECTOR **Fabien Baron**
PUBLISHER **Condé Nast International, Inc.**
CATEGORY **Single Page/Spread**
DATE **February 1988**

PUBLICATION **Italian Vogue**
ART DIRECTOR **Fabien Baron**
PUBLISHER **Condé Nast International, Inc.**
CATEGORY **Single Page/Spread**
DATE **February 1988**

PUBLICATION **Italian Vogue**
ART DIRECTOR **Fabien Baron**
PHOTOGRAPHER **Satoshi**
PUBLISHER **Condé Nast International, Inc.**
CATEGORY **Single Page/Spread**
DATE **September 1988**

PUBLICATION **Italian Vogue**
ART DIRECTOR **Fabien Baron**
PHOTOGRAPHER **Steven Meisel**
PUBLISHER **Condé Nast International, Inc.**
CATEGORY **Single Page/Spread**
DATE **September 1988**

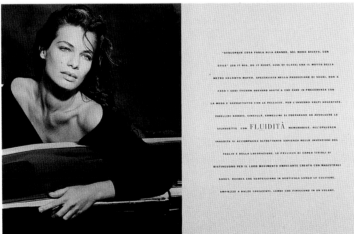

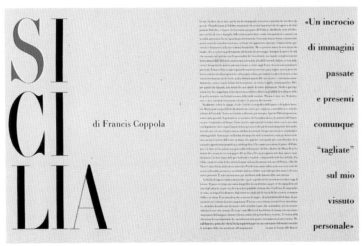

PUBLICATION **Italian Vogue**
ART DIRECTOR **Fabien Baron**
PHOTOGRAPHER **Albert Watson**
PUBLISHER **Condé Nast International, Inc.**
CATEGORY **Single Page/Spread**
DATE **November 1988**

PUBLICATION **Italian Vogue**
ART DIRECTOR **Fabien Baron**
DESIGNER **Lucia Stoppini**
PUBLISHER **Condé Nast International, Inc.**
CATEGORY **Single Page/Spread**
DATE **December 1988**

PUBLICATION **San Francisco Focus**
ART DIRECTOR **Matthew Drace**
DESIGNER **Matthew Drace**
PHOTOGRAPHER **Geof Kern**
PUBLISHER **KQED, Inc.**
CATEGORY **Single Page/Spread**
DATE **June 1988**

PUBLICATION **San Francisco Focus**
ART DIRECTOR **Matthew Drace**
DESIGNER **Hazel Boissiere**
ILLUSTRATOR **Bart de Haas**
PUBLISHER **KQED, Inc.**
CATEGORY **Single Page/Spread**
DATE **October 1988**

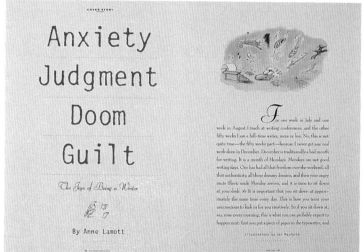

PUBLICATION **San Francisco Focus**
ART DIRECTOR **Matthew Drace**
DESIGNER **Mark Ulriksen**
ILLUSTRATOR **Hal Mayforth**
PUBLISHER **KQED, Inc.**
CATEGORY **Single Page/Spread**
DATE **April 1988**

PUBLICATION **Italian Vogue**
ART DIRECTOR **Fabien Baron**
PHOTOGRAPHER **Albert Watson, G. Bruno Casolaro**
PUBLISHER **Condé Nast International, Inc.**
CATEGORY **Single Page/Spread**
DATE **November 1988**

PUBLICATION **Italian Vogue**
ART DIRECTOR **Fabien Baron**
PUBLISHER **Condé Nast International, Inc.**
CATEGORY **Single Page/Spread**
DATE **September 1988**

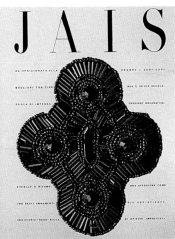

PUBLICATION **Italian Vogue**
ART DIRECTOR **Fabien Baron**
PHOTOGRAPHER **Andrew McPherson**
PUBLISHER **Condé Nast International, Inc.**
CATEGORY **Single Page/Spread**
DATE **November 1988**

PUBLICATION **Italian Vogue**
ART DIRECTOR **Fabien Baron**
PHOTOGRAPHER **David Hockney**
PUBLISHER **Condé Nast International, Inc.**
CATEGORY **Single Page/Spread**
DATE **November 1988**

PUBLICATION **Metropolis**
ART DIRECTOR **Helene Silverman**
DESIGNER **Helene Silverman**
PHOTOGRAPHER **Mark Sullo**
PUBLISHER **Bellerophon Publications**
CATEGORY **Single Page/Spread**
DATE **March 1988**

PUBLICATION **Metropolis**
ART DIRECTOR **Helene Silverman**
DESIGNER **Jeff Christensen**
PUBLISHER **Bellerophon Publications**
CATEGORY **Single Page/Spread**
DATE **July/August 1988**

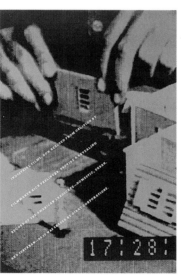

PUBLICATION **Metropolis**
ART DIRECTOR **Helene Silverman**
DESIGNER **Helene Silverman**
PUBLISHER **Bellerophon Publications**
CATEGORY **Single Page/Spread**
DATE **May 1988**

PUBLICATION **Metropolis**
ART DIRECTOR **Helene Silverman**
DESIGNER **Helene Silverman**
PHOTOGRAPHER **Daniel Levy**
PUBLISHER **Bellerophon Publications**
CATEGORY **Single Page/Spread**
DATE **November 1988**

PUBLICATION **Regardies**
ART DIRECTOR **John Korpics**
DESIGNER **John Korpics**
ILLUSTRATOR **Matt Mahurin**
PUBLISHER **Regardies, Inc.**
CATEGORY **Single Page/Spread**
DATE **November 1988**

PUBLICATION **Access**
ART DIRECTOR **Bryan Peterson**
DESIGNER **Bryan Peterson**
ILLUSTRATOR **Melissa Grimes**
CLIENT **Northern Telecom**
AGENCY **Peterson & Company, Dallas, TX**
CATEGORY **Single Page/Spread**
DATE **Fall 1988**

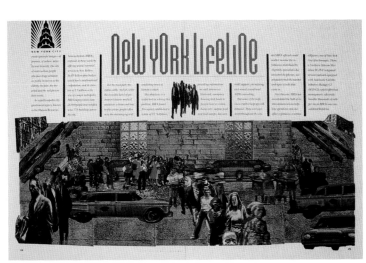

PUBLICATION **Rolling Stone**
ART DIRECTOR **Fred Woodward**
DESIGNER **Jolene Cuyler**
ILLUSTRATOR **Brian Cronin**
PUBLISHER **Straight Arrow Publishers**
CATEGORY **Single Page/Spread**
DATE **November 17, 1988**

PUBLICATION **Access**
ART DIRECTOR **Bryan Peterson**
DESIGNER **Bryan Peterson**
PHOTOGRAPHER **Ellen Schuster**
CLIENT **Northern Telecom**
AGENCY **Peterson & Company, Dallas, TX**
CATEGORY **Single Page/Spread**
DATE **Fall 1988**

PUBLICATION **How**
ART DIRECTOR **Scott Menchin**
DESIGNER **Scott Menchin**
PHOTOGRAPHER **Franklin Avery**
PUBLISHER **F & W Publications**
CATEGORY **Single Page/Spread**
DATE **November/December 1988**

PUBLICATION **How**
ART DIRECTOR **Scott Menchin**
DESIGNER **Scott Menchin**
PHOTOGRAPHER **William Duke**
PUBLISHER **F & W Publications**
CATEGORY **Single Page/Spread**
DATE **November/December 1988**

PUBLICATION **How**
ART DIRECTOR **Scott Menchin**
DESIGNER **Scott Menchin**
PUBLISHER **F & W Publications**
CATEGORY **Single Page/Spread**
DATE **July/August 1988**

56

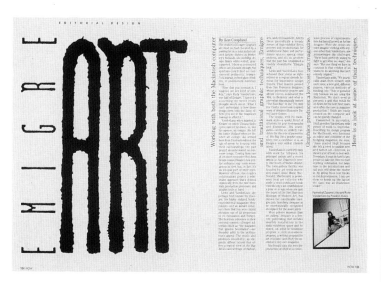

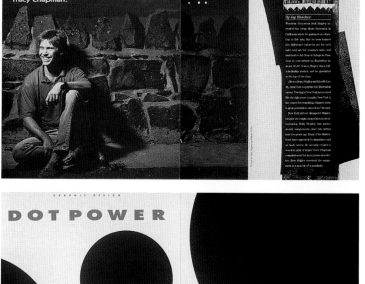

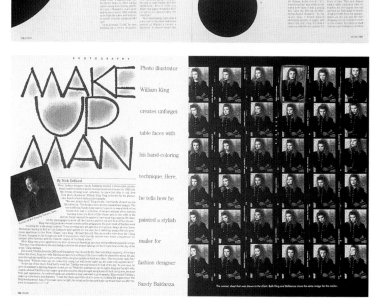

PUBLICATION **How**
ART DIRECTOR **Scott Menchin**
DESIGNER **Scott Menchin**
ILLUSTRATOR **Peter Kuper**
PHOTOGRAPHER **William Duke**
PUBLISHER **F & W Publications**
CATEGORY **Single Page/Spread**
DATE **November/December 1988**

PUBLICATION **How**
ART DIRECTOR **Scott Menchin**
DESIGNER **Scott Menchin**
PHOTOGRAPHER **Sato, Bill King**
PUBLISHER **F & W Publications**
CATEGORY **Single Page/Spread**
DATE **September/October 1988**

PUBLICATION **BandWagon**
ART DIRECTOR **Jan Wilson**
DESIGNER **Jan Wilson**
PHOTOGRAPHER **Neill Whitlock**
CLIENT **Frito-Lay, Inc.**
AGENCY **Peterson & Company, Dallas, TX**
CATEGORY **Single Page/Spread**
DATE **Summer 1988**

PUBLICATION **LA Business**
ART DIRECTOR **Michael Walters**
DESIGNER **Michael Walters**
PHOTOGRAPHER **Alan Levenson, Wider Archive**
PUBLISHER **California Business News, Inc.**
CATEGORY **Single Page/Spread**
DATE **October 1988**

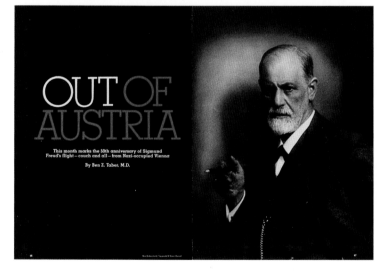

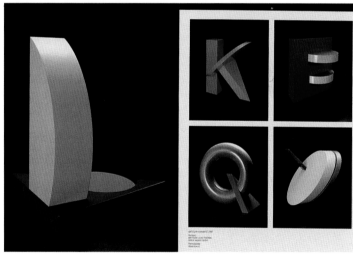

PUBLICATION **MD Magazine**
ART DIRECTOR **Al Foti**
DESIGNER **Al Foti**
PHOTOGRAPHER **Max Halberstadt**
PUBLISHER **MD Publications, Inc.**
CATEGORY **Single Page/Spread**
DATE **June 1988**

PUBLICATION **Graphis**
ART DIRECTOR **B. Martin Pedersen**
DESIGNER **B. Martin Pedersen**
PUBLISHER **Graphis Publishing Corporation**
CATEGORY **Single Page/Spread**
DATE **April 1988**

PUBLICATION **Studio**
ART DIRECTOR **Alfredo Muccino**
DESIGNER **Alfredo Muccino**
PHOTOGRAPHER **Franklyn Avery**
CLIENT **Western Art Directors Club**
AGENCY **Muccino Design Group, San Jose, CA**
CATEGORY **Single Page/Spread**
DATE **June 1988**

PUBLICATION **Town & Country Annual Report**
ART DIRECTOR **Richard Tesoro**
CLIENT **The Hearst Corporation**
AGENCY **Parham, Santana Design, Inc., NYC**
CATEGORY **Single Page/Spread**
DATE **Summer 1988**

PUBLICATION **Egghead**
DESIGN DIRECTOR **John Zimmerman**
ART DIRECTOR **Karen Gutowsky**
PHOTOGRAPHER **David Carter**
CLIENT **Egghead Discount Software**
AGENCY **Z Group, Seattle, WA**
CATEGORY **Single Page/Spread**
DATE **July/August 1988**

PUBLICATION **Archiforum**
DESIGN DIRECTOR **Mark Oliver**
DESIGNER **Susan Edelmann-Adams**
CLIENT **Berkus Group Architects**
AGENCY **Marc Oliver, Inc., Santa Barbara, CA**
CATEGORY **Single Page/Spread**
DATE **Winter 1988**

PUBLICATION **Caring**
ART DIRECTOR **Mark Geer**
DESIGNER **Mark Geer**
ILLUSTRATOR **Brad Holland**
CLIENT **Memorial Care Systems**
AGENCY **Mark Geer Design, Houston, TX**
CATEGORY **Single Page/Spread**
DATE **Summer/Fall 1988**

PUBLICATION **Caring**
ART DIRECTOR **Mark Geer**
DESIGNER **Mark Geer**
ILLUSTRATOR **Melissa Grimes**
CLIENT **Memorial Care Systems**
AGENCY **Mark Geer Design, Houston, TX**
CATEGORY **Single Page/Spread**
DATE **Summer/Fall 1988**

PUBLICATION **Computer Systems News**
DESIGN DIRECTOR **Joe McNeill**
ART DIRECTOR **Nicole White**
PHOTOGRAPHER **Danuta Otfinowski**
PUBLISHER **CMP Publications**
CATEGORY **Single Page/Spread**
DATE **November 14, 1988**

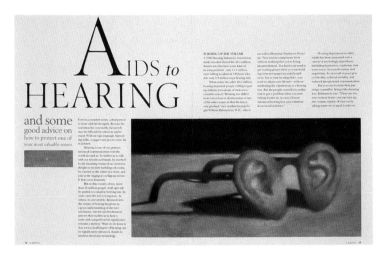

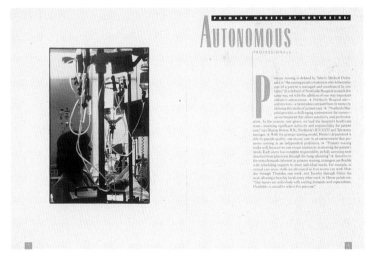

PUBLICATION **Caring**
ART DIRECTOR **Mark Geer**
DESIGNER **Mark Geer**
PHOTOGRAPHER **Mike Hallaway**
CLIENT **Memorial Care Systems**
AGENCY **Mark Geer Design, Houston, TX**
CATEGORY **Single Page/Spread**
DATE **Summer/Fall 1988**

PUBLICATION **Northside Nurse**
ART DIRECTOR **Barbara Cohen**
DESIGNER **Barbara Cohen**
PHOTOGRAPHER **Anne States**
CLIENT **Northside Hospital**
AGENCY **Cohen & Co., Atlanta, GA**
CATEGORY **Single Page/Spread**
DATE **First Quarter 1988**

PUBLICATION **Computer Systems News**
DESIGN DIRECTOR **Joe McNeill**
ART DIRECTOR **Nicole White**
PHOTOGRAPHER **Danuta Otfinowski**
PUBLISHER **CMP Publications**
CATEGORY **Single Page/Spread**
DATE **November 14, 1988**

PUBLICATION **The New York Times Travel Section**
ART DIRECTOR **Michael Valenti**
DESIGNER **Michael Valenti**
ILLUSTRATOR **Bob Gale**
PHOTOGRAPHER **Herlinde Koelbl, Jonathan Player**
PUBLISHER **The New York Times**
CATEGORY **Single Page/Spread**
DATE **October 10, 1988**

PUBLICATION **DNR International**
ART DIRECTOR **Lynette Cortez**
DESIGNER **Lynette Cortez**
PUBLISHER **Fairchild Publications**
CATEGORY **Single Page/Spread**
DATE **March 1988**

PUBLICATION **The Washington Post**
ART DIRECTOR **Nancy Brooke Smith**
DESIGNER **Nancy Brooke Smith**
ILLUSTRATOR **Phil Huling**
PUBLISHER **The Washington Post**
CATEGORY **Single Page/Spread**
DATE **April 27, 1988**

PUBLICATION **The New York Times Travel Special**
ART DIRECTOR **Michael Valenti**
DESIGNER **Michael Valenti**
ILLUSTRATOR **Jean Tuttle**
PUBLISHER **The New York Times**
CATEGORY **Single Page/Spread**
DATE **March 6, 1988**

PUBLICATION **The New York Times Travel Section**
ART DIRECTOR **Michael Valenti**
DESIGNER **Michael Valenti**
ILLUSTRATOR **Steven Guarnaccia**
PUBLISHER **The New York Times**
CATEGORY **Single Page/Spread**
DATE **April 10, 1988**

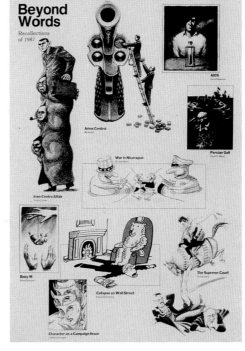

PUBLICATION **The New York Times Travel Section**
ART DIRECTOR **Michael Valenti**
DESIGNER **Michael Valenti**
ILLUSTRATOR **Douglas Smith**
PHOTOGRAPHER **Herlinde Koelbl, Brian Payne**
PUBLISHER **The New York Times**
CATEGORY **Single Page/Spread**
DATE **August 7, 1988**

PUBLICATION **The New York Times Week in Review**
ART DIRECTOR **John Cayea**
DESIGNER **John Cayea**
PUBLISHER **The New York Times**
CATEGORY **Single Page/Spread**
DATE **January 26, 1988**

PUBLICATION **GQ**
ART DIRECTOR **Robert Priest**
DESIGNER **Alejandro Gonzalez**
PHOTOGRAPHER **Matthew Rolston**
PUBLISHER **Condé Nast Publications, Inc.**
CATEGORY **Story Presentation**
DATE **December 1988**

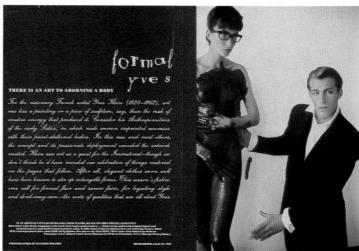

PUBLICATION **Life, 150 Years of Photography**
DESIGN DIRECTOR **Tom Bentkowski**
ART DIRECTOR **Nora Sheehan**
PHOTOGRAPHER **Irving Penn**
PUBLISHER **Time, Inc.**
CATEGORY **Story Presentation**
DATE **Fall 1988**

PUBLICATION **Philadelphia**
ART DIRECTOR **Ken Newbaker**
DESIGNER **Patricia Mc El Roy**
PHOTOGRAPHER **Mary D'Anella**
PUBLISHER **Metrocorp**
CATEGORY **Story Presentation**
DATE **December 1988**

PUBLICATION **Life, 150 Years of Photography**
DESIGN DIRECTOR **Tom Bentkowski**
ART DIRECTOR **Nora Sheehan**
DESIGNER **Nora Sheehan**
PUBLISHER **Time, Inc.**
CATEGORY **Story Presentation**
DATE **Fall 1988**

PUBLICATION **Spy**
ART DIRECTOR **Alexander Isley**
DESIGNER **Alexander Knowlton**
ILLUSTRATOR **Natasha Lessnik**
PHOTO EDITOR **Amy Stark**
PUBLISHER **Spy Publishing**
CATEGORY **Story Presentation**
DATE **April 1988**

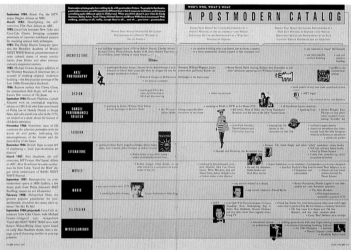

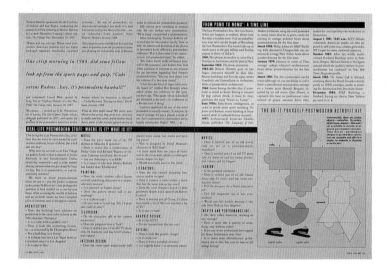

CITY OF ANGELS

PHOTOGRAPHS BY DAVID STRICK

DAVID STRICK is the third generation of a Hollywood family. His great-uncle, the director Herbert Biberman, and great-aunt, the actress Gale Sondergaard, were both blacklisted during the McCarthy era. Strick's father is an Academy Award-winning producer and director, and his mother is a film publicist. One of Strick's childhood memories is of Rona Barrett reporting his parents' divorce proceedings on television. Sixty-five of his photographs will be published later this year by the Atlantic Monthly Press in *Our Hollywood*, Strick's first book.

Hollywood

Much of what is written about pictures and about picture people approaches reality only occasionally and accidentally. *Joan Didion, The White Album, 1979*

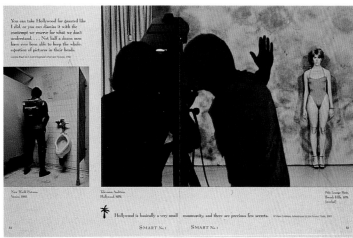

You can take Hollywood for granted like I did, or you can dismiss it with the contempt we reserve for what we don't understand.... Not half a dozen men have ever been able to keep the whole equation of pictures in their heads. *Cecil Beaton of Scott Fitzgerald's The Last Tycoon, 1941*

New World Pictures. Venice, 1986.

Television Audition. Hollywood, 1976.

Polo Lounge Patio. Beverly Hills, 1978. *(partial)*

Hollywood is basically a very small community, and there are precious few secrets. *William Goldman, Adventures in the Screen Trade, 1983*

Universal Studios Mako Tour. Universal City, 1976.

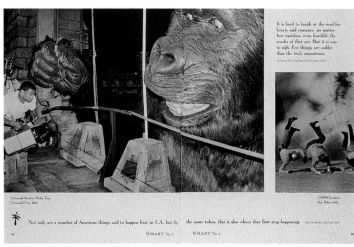

It is hard to laugh at the need for beauty and romance, no matter how tasteless, even horrible, the results of that are. But it is easy to sigh. Few things are sadder than the truly monstrous. *Nathanael West, The Day of the Locust, 1939*

CHIPS London. Sun Pedro, 1982.

Not only are a number of American things said to happen first in L.A., but, by the same token, that is also where they first stop happening. *Larry McMurtry, Film Flam, 1987*

SMART No. 1   SMART No. 1

PUBLICATION **Smart**
ART DIRECTOR **Janet Waegel**
DESIGNER **Roger Black**
PHOTOGRAPHER **David Strick**
PUBLISHER **Smart American, Inc.**
CATEGORY **Story Presentation**
DATE **Fall 1988**

PUBLICATION **Texas Monthly**
ART DIRECTOR **D.J. Stout**
DESIGNER **D.J. Stout**
PHOTOGRAPHER **Geof Kern**
PUBLISHER **Texas Monthly**
CATEGORY **Story Presentation**
DATE **January 1988**

THE SINS OF WALKER RAILEY

I had to know, did the minister of the church I grew up in try to murder his wife? I told him I thought he was guilty. "I hear what you're saying," he said.

by Lawrence Wright

THE SINS OF WALKER RAILEY

Peggy was neither dead nor alive—it was as if the were waiting for some momentous resolution before she could either die or be released back into life.

NEWSREEL

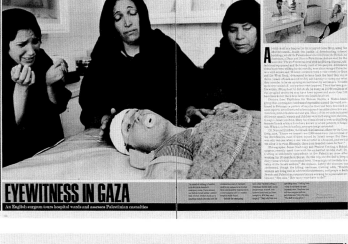

EYEWITNESS IN GAZA

An English surgeon tours hospital wards and assesses Palestinian casualties

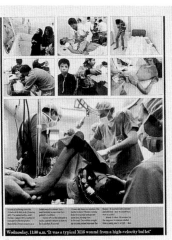

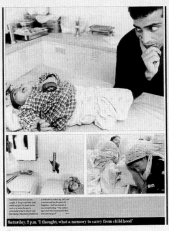

Wednesday, 11:30 a.m. "It was a typical M16 wound from a high-velocity bullet"

Saturday, 2 p.m. "I thought, what a memory to carry from childhood"

PUBLICATION **Life**
ART DIRECTOR **Tom Bentkowski**
DESIGNER **Tom Bentkowski**
PHOTOGRAPHER **James Nachtwey**
PHOTO EDITOR **Peter Howe**
PUBLISHER **Time, Inc.**
CATEGORY **Story Presentation**
DATE **June 1988**

PUBLICATION **Life**
ART DIRECTOR **Tom Bentkowski**
DESIGNER **Robin E. Brown**
PHOTOGRAPHER **Herman Le Roy Emmet**
PUBLISHER **Time, Inc.**
CATEGORY **Story Presentation**
DATE **December 1988**

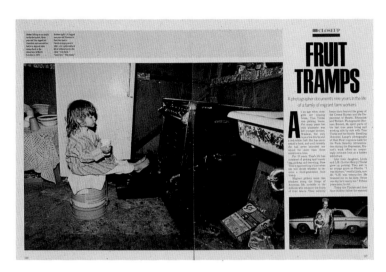

PUBLICATION **Life**
ART DIRECTOR **Tom Bentkowski**
DESIGNER **Nora Sheehan**
PHOTOGRAPHER **Gilles Peress**
PUBLISHER **Time, Inc.**
CATEGORY **Story Presentation**
DATE **May 1988**

PUBLICATION **Life**
ART DIRECTOR **Tom Bentkowski**
DESIGNER **Nora Sheehan**
PUBLISHER **Time, Inc.**
CATEGORY **Story Presentation**
DATE **March 1988**

■ PORTFOLIO

A forbidden look at
the outcasts who are building
a highway 12,400 feet
in the sky

On the Road

■ PICTURE ESSAY

CITY OF LOST BOYS

Driven from Sudan's
farms and villages by
civil war, famine and
poverty, some 10,000
children scratch out a
precarious existence on
the streets of Khartoum

PUBLICATION **Life**
ART DIRECTOR **Tom Bentkowski**
DESIGNER **Robin E. Brown**
PHOTOGRAPHER **Mary Ellen Mark**
PUBLISHER **Time, Inc.**
CATEGORY **Story Presentation**
DATE **June 1988**

PUBLICATION **Life**
ART DIRECTOR **Tom Bentkowski**
DESIGNER **Tom Bentkowski**
PHOTOGRAPHER **Sebastiao Salgado**
PUBLISHER **Time, Inc.**
CATEGORY **Story Presentation**
DATE **August 1988**

▬ PORTFOLIO

FOUR CENTURIES OF HARVESTING SUGAR

CUBA

Photographer Sebastiao Salgado captures the toil and camaraderie in the country's cane fields

His documentation of vanishing ways of work has now taken Salgado to a sugar plantation near Havana. First cultivated in the late 1500s, sugarcane accounts for 75 percent of Cuba's exports. Though the industry has been mechanized since the 1959 revolution, a third of the crop still is harvested by hand. From December through May, 100,000 men slash from sunrise to sunset. Most leave regular jobs for the fields. The pay is better than the national average of $180 a month, and the labor is considered patriotic. "They believe the worker is the real base of their system," says Salgado. A man can cut 5,000 pounds of cane in eight hours. A machine does three times that amount in 15 minutes. Clearly, the days of the machete-wielding army are numbered.

The technique—stoop and slash—and the tools are still the same. "These men love the macho ambience," says Salgado, "and the cutting."

Tractors and oxen are used to scoop up felled cane. Fields are burned the night before harvest to rid the cane of leaves—goggles are worn because of ash and cinder.

Reaming a rum distiller, a man comes up for air. A 1915 U.S.-made steam locomotive conveys the crop to the mills. From coastal terminals bags of sugar leave for the U.S.S.R.

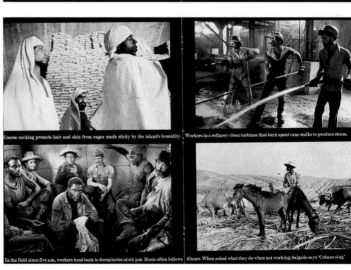

Coarse sacking protects hair and skin from sugar made sticky by the island's humidity. Workers in a refinery clean turbines that burn spent cane stalks to produce steam.

In the field since five a.m., workers head back to dormitories at six p.m. Music often follows dinner. When asked what they do when not working, Salgado says: "Cubans sing."

PORTFOLIO

A TRIBUTE TO A VANISHING WAY OF
WORK

In a rare visit to Soviet factories, a photojournalist embarks on a labor of love

Sebastiao Salgado is in a race against time and technology. "There is an irreversible process taking place around the world, and it is happening faster than we think," says the 44-year-old photographer, speaking in the staccato bursts of a man in a hurry. "In ten or fifteen years, these pictures will be part of history." Salgado believes that computers and robots have delivered a "brutal shock" to the methods of production and "man no longer sees the fruits of his work." With missionary zeal, Salgado has begun to document the last vestige of a kind of labor that puts man in intimate contact with the product he creates. The photographs on the following pages, taken in a steel plant and an auto factory in Zaporozhye, a city of 863,000 in the Soviet Ukraine, are the initial dispatches of a three-year venture that will take Salgado around the globe. Future projects will include sugarcane fields in Cuba, chemical factories in West Germany, cotton fields in China, tin mines in Bolivia and limestone quarries in Indiana. "What I hope to achieve is a world portrait of a disappearing race, the working-class man," he says.

The son of a Brazilian cattle rancher, Salgado moved to Paris in 1969, where he earned a master's degree in economics. In 1973, as an economist for the International Coffee Organization in Africa, he found he was more interested in taking pictures than in filling out production reports. So he quit to make a career with a camera. "I could have photographed landscapes, but what interests me is something more basic and human. It is a struggle for dignity." In this, Salgado's images are in the tradition of W. Eugene Smith, the master of the photo essay, whom Salgado considers his major influence. "He had an enormous respect for people," says Salgado. Ten years ago Sebastiao visited a steel plant in France. The worker there "was strong; he had muscle; he was resistant," says Salgado. "Today it is an intellectual who makes steel." Indeed, a few weeks after he finished photographing at the Zaporozhye auto factory, the plant began installing robots.

119

A Zaporozhye steel plant worker, visored for protection against sparks, positions vats of molten ore. Says Salgado, "It's a dangerous profession. You have to concentrate all the time."

Every two hours the assembly line stops for 15 minutes and the workers break for tea or a card game. "It is a very human atmosphere. The factory is a part of their social life."

Until last December the city's auto plant assembled 150,000 subcompacts a year. "The cars were virtually hand-built. This woman's job was to solder exhaust pipes to gas tanks."

PUBLICATION **Life**
ART DIRECTOR **Tom Bentkowski**
DESIGNER **Tom Bentkowski**
PHOTOGRAPHER **Sebastiao Salgado**
PUBLISHER **Time, Inc.**
CATEGORY **Story Presentation**
DATE **May 1988**

PUBLICATION **Life**
ART DIRECTOR **Tom Bentkowski**
DESIGNER **Robin Brown**
PHOTOGRAPHER **James Nachtwey**
PHOTO EDITOR **Peter Howe**
PUBLISHER **Time, Inc.**
CATEGORY **Story Presentation**
DATE **November 1988**

LIFE

AN EXCLUSIVE
LOOK INSIDE THE
SOVIET ARMY
BY ROY ROWAN

BOOT CAMP

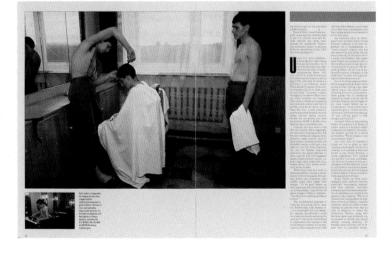

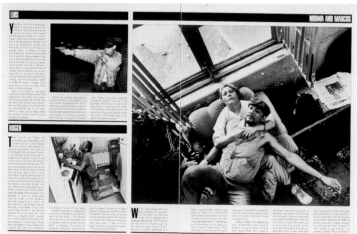

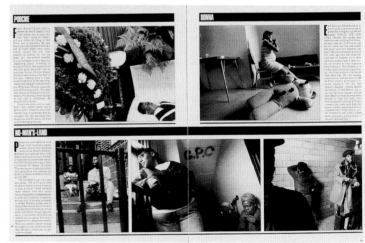

72

PUBLICATION **Life**
ART DIRECTOR **Tom Bentkowski**
DESIGNER **Tom Bentkowski**
PHOTOGRAPHER **Eugene Richards**
PHOTO EDITOR **Peter Howe**
PUBLISHER **Time, Inc.**
CATEGORY **Story Presentation**
DATE **July 1988**

PUBLICATION **Life**
ART DIRECTOR **Tom Bentkowski**
DESIGNER **Tom Bentkowski**
PHOTOGRAPHER **Alon Reininger**
PUBLISHER **Time, Inc.**
CATEGORY **Story Presentation**
DATE **January 1988**

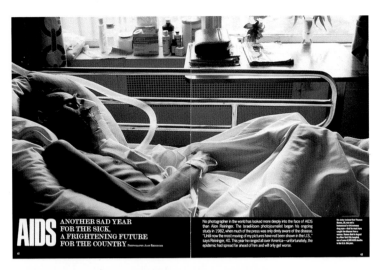

AIDS ANOTHER SAD YEAR FOR THE SICK, A FRIGHTENING FUTURE FOR THE COUNTRY

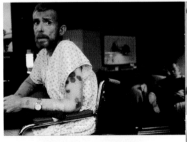

PUBLICATION **Life**
ART DIRECTOR **Tom Bentkowski**
DESIGNER **Robin E. Brown**
PHOTOGRAPHER **Harold Feinstein**
PUBLISHER **Time, Inc.**
CATEGORY **Story Presentation**
DATE **August 1988**

PUBLICATION **Life**
DESIGN DIRECTOR **Tom Bentkowski**
ART DIRECTOR **Nora Sheehan**
DESIGNER **Nora Sheehan**
PUBLISHER **Time, Inc.**
CATEGORY **Story Presentation**
DATE **Fall 1988**

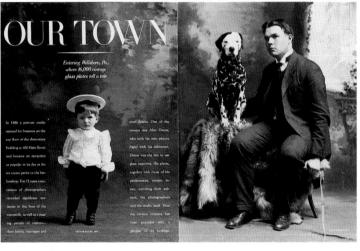

GAME SHOW

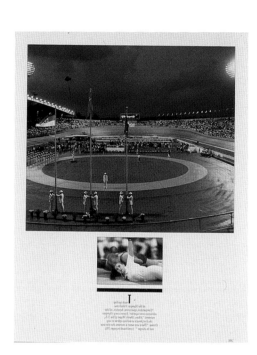

PUBLICATION **Life**
ART DIRECTOR **Tom Bentkowski**
DESIGNER **Nora Sheehan**
PHOTOGRAPHER **David Burnett**
PUBLISHER **Time, Inc.**
CATEGORY **Story Presentation**
DATE **March 1988**

76

PUBLICATION **Life**
ART DIRECTOR **Tom Bentkowski**
DESIGNER **Nora Sheehan**
PHOTOGRAPHER **Walter Iooss**
PUBLISHER **Time, Inc.**
CATEGORY **Story Presentation**
DATE **February 1988**

SPORTS

Goldrush '88

Winter Canada is bracing for an arctic high; the exhilaration of some 1,700 Olympians from 58 nations vying for winter gold. The Games, which open on February 13 in Calgary, are the longest and most expensive to date. They have been stretched from 12 to 16 days to accommodate television (ABC paid a record $300 million for U.S. rights alone), and $1 billion has been spent to prepare for athletes, spectators—and even the weather. Should a warm chinook wind begin blowing, workers are poised to combat meltdown with tons of banked snow and a phalanx of machines that make the artificial variety. The 156-member Team America will do well to top the U.S. Winter

Games average of three golds, three silvers and two bronzes. In a nation where most of the playing fields are warm and level, a few of the 46 medal events of the Winter Games are downright alien. All of America's various biathletes could flambeard a 747, and one congressman recently asked if the luge was an edible fish (ahem, it's a sled). The high-profile ski team, winner of five medals in 1984, has been racked by injuries. Still, the Americans on these pages, among them a biathlete, a luger, two figure skaters, a bobsledder and skating speedster Bonnie Blair (cover and page 86), have realistic medal hopes. So dial up the thermostat, align the antenna—and let the Games begin.

NICK THOMETZ

MATT ROI

DEBI THOMAS

BRIAN BOITANO

THE SIGHT FANTASTIC

Using their street smarts, a gang of daring kids from Canada is turning the circus into a saucy new art form.

C ircuses come and go in Washington, D.C., but they've always included donkeys and elephants. Now there's a circus captivating the capital that has an animal cast all—just 32 marvelously exuberant and gutsy acrobats, trick bicyclists, clowns, teeterboard flippers, jugglers and aerialists. Created four years ago as part of Canada's 450th anniversary celebration, the Montreal-based Cirque du Soleil (Circus of the Sun) barely qualifies as a big top; its blue and yellow tent has only one ring and seats just 1,756 spectators. Most of the troupe started out as sidewalk performers. For example, hand balancer Amélie Demay signed on after the Cirque's artistic director saw her spinning on her head at a Quebec street festival. Contortionist Angela Laurier first honed her skills on the pavements of Montreal and later toured Europe with the Sidewalk Circus of Brussels. "On the street," says Laurier, "you learn to be fast and theatrical. You have to be able to surprise and captivate passersby." In the beginning, the government picked up all the annual operating costs; today the circus is nearly self-supporting, with a $14 million annual budget. Last September the troupe crossed the border—and Yanks

went bonkers. In San Francisco, director Francis Coppola loved the show so much he threw a party for the entire ensemble, including the crew. Steve Martin, who knows all about being funny, declared master clown Denis Lacombe a genius. In L.A. scalpers hawked $19.50 tickets, the most expensive seats, for 10 times that much. And in New York the show was held over five weeks.

Everywhere critics raved about the zany humor, the colorful bespangled costumes and the high-tech production. Indeed, every act is precisely choreographed, and there is a five-piece orchestra to provide an original, pulsating accompaniment that is as fused with the action as a movie sound track. "What's really special about the Cirque," says Lacombe, who idolizes Buster Keaton and Disney's Donald Duck and Goofy, "is that we went back to the roots of the circus 200 years ago and brought it into the 1980s."

PUBLICATION **Life**
ART DIRECTOR **Tom Bentkowski**
DESIGNER **Tom Bentkowski**
PHOTOGRAPHER **Walter Iooss**
PUBLISHER **Time, Inc.**
CATEGORY **Story Presentation**
DATE **October 1988**

78

PUBLICATION **Life**
DESIGN DIRECTOR **Tom Bentkowski**
ART DIRECTOR **Nora Sheehan**
DESIGNER **Nora Sheehan, Tom Bentkowski**
PHOTOGRAPHER **Weston, Bresson, Atget, Stieglitz, Cameron, Evans, Adams**
AGENCY **Time, Inc.**
PUBLISHER **Story Presentation**
CATEGORY **Fall 1988**

WESTON

NUDE, 1925

CARTIER-BRESSON

HYÈRES, FRANCE, 1932

As a boy, Edward Weston (1864-1958) saved his pennies to buy secondhand camera equipment. By 21 he had a studio in Tropico, Calif., and was affecting the role of artist by wearing a velvet cape. His romantic, soft-focus pictures, indeed, won him worldwide recognition. But in 1915 he saw a exhibit of modern art, including his work... He then adopted "straight photography." His subjects—shells, cypress roots, peppers, a toilet bowl, nudes—each photographed as it looked like in common. As sitgman Weston wrote, "The camera should be used for recording the very substance and quintessence of the thing itself, whether it be polished steel or palpitating flesh." Critic Susan Sontag said even more: "The peppers Weston photographed are voluptuous in a way his female nudes rarely are. In fact, he made nudes sexless; sexless, respectable." That's Weston's own show.

Henri Cartier-Bresson was born in 1908 near Paris. His father was a wealthy textile manufacturer. As the child viewed an uncle's studio, and so became his passion. "I inhaled the camera," he recalled. At 24 he got a Leica, and photography replaced painting as his obsession. He traveled to Spain, Mexico and Italy, and with his camera "strived to seize the whole essence, in the confines of a single photograph." After World War II he turned to photojournalism with what one critic described as "a more lyrical narrative style." In 1973 with a famous series, "When faces on his feet, he has no equal" catching what he likes. "Can the decisive moment be the very "the decisive moment," to which he "continually fixed a geometric pattern without which the photograph would be both formless and lifeless." He added: "There are no rare times in the world; I'm not only ever a few geometry."

ATGET

STIEGLITZ

ORGAN GRINDER, 1899

RAINY NIGHT, NEW YORK, 1897

Eugène Atget (1857-1927) was orphaned at a child, became a sailor, then toured provincial France as a bit player in a two-bit theatrical troupe. At 40 he abandoned the stage and became a painter—barely and unsuccessful. About 1898, Atget picked up a camera for the first time and began to photograph "everything in Paris and its environs that was artistic and picturesque." His primitive approach yielded more than 10,000 photographs, from alleys to street lamps, garbage collectors to shop keepers. Fellow photographer Berenice Abbott wrote, "He was an intense, histrionic, a Balzac of the camera, from whose work we can learn a large tapestry of French civilization." Soon Edward Schlemz, attempt at George Eastman House, "One has the feeling with Atget that he wasn't concerned whether what he was doing was art. He was just making good photographs."

Stieglitz of a prosperous New York woolens importer, Alfred Stieglitz (1864-1946) went to Germany in 1881 to study mechanical engineering but played hilltum and went to the stacks instead. Once January day that he knew he said to see have been persuaded, he bought a camera for $7.50. Soon he was spending 10-hour shifts in the Berlin darkroom, photographing while it was in the dark. The report, walking at times at 100 times of straight kook said, "but theseit understate mutations, his life itself." His ferocious publications continued and to his New York gallery, where he displayed the works of fine new artists. But with war Georgia O'Keeffe], much his, saw Weston.] Next picture in the J. Paul Getty Museum, "one of the most important artist-photographers the corolla but new products," said Stieglitz. "Photography is my passion. The search for truth is my obsession."

CAMERON

EVANS

ALICE LIDDELL, 1872

GENERAL STORE, MOUNDVILLE, ALA., 1936

Julia Margaret Cameron (1815-1879) got her first camera, a gift from her daughter, when she was 48. Nonetheless, says photo historian Beaumont Newhall, Cameron's "dynamic portraits are among the most noble and impressive yet produced." Married to a well-to-do British lover, Cameron photographed such well-known personalities as writers Ellen Terry, scientist Charles Darwin and cousin's niece of Bloomsbury. But the Leeming Clent Sonic Hen son was making low class pitiful portraiture our poet "sweet untamed sugar graphic photographs—most moving and unkempt any dangling of bustle and blouse." To those who suggested at her miniature prints less blurred, "Why have right to say what focus is the appearance Social?" said, uh-huh. "My appearances are to touch Me Photography and so cry from the character and create at High Art by combining the real & idea."

Walker Evans (1903-1975) went to Williams College for one year and then to the Sorbonne. In 1930 he began a lifetime's search to let Flaubert's motto and focus to the agrarian Social?" said, critic, "I know what I want, I say photograph comes from the back of a moving car. If it is clean, it is later." Critic Hilton Kramer wrote of his work, "Many of his pictures are now a standard of social decay or abandoned exploitation. Evans one sees raising poetry, everything to be unheated used some Model T's and America's poet Emma Lincoln Kirstein wrote that Evans's pictures "are so full of facts they have to be supposed with more than just facts." He flat the illustrations for James Agee's unforgettable Let Us Now Praise Famous Men, but Evans was always master-of-fact about his art.

ADAMS

WINTER SUNRISE, SIERRA NEVADA, FROM LONE PINE, 1944

Ansel Adams (1902-1984) grew up in San Francisco, a hyperactive child rumored at home. In 1916 his father took him to Yosemite. Ansel had his Brownie camera along, and he returned to the mountains at least once a year for the next 60. In 1930 he saw Paul Strand's work and recognized fresh possibilities in photography. Then, forming Group f/64 with Edward Weston, Imogen Cunningham and others, Adams had "a new vision, the crest of a wave." A superb technician, his grand landscapes are utterly distinctive works, and critic Robert Hughes said of him, "Adams's entire career represented a restrained, meticulous effort to order the jumble of the natural world; its colors, its erratic tones and shifting values, into a precisely turned structure of differing greys." Trained as a pianist, Adams said that when he saw a fine print, "sometimes I hear music—Bach, Chopin ..."

A·M·E·R·I·C·A·N
WONDER

TEXT BY TONY SWAN

When the automobile rolled onto the world stage, 102 years ago, there were no schools of design – only a drawing industry drawing freely on the technologies of its centuries-old predecessors. Consequently, it was no accident that early automobiles looked very much like carriages. The early carmakers worked within an existing discipline, subordinating the unproven but vast potential of the internal combustion engine for the slow and messy reliability of the horse. ● Gottlieb Daimler and Karl Benz are generally credited with launching the automotive era in 1886. Even though a number of U.S. manufacturers were busy with their own interpretations of this new idea well before the turn of the century, it was some time before anyone on

WHEELS

PHOTOGRAPHS BY HENRY WOLF

this side of the Atlantic commanded much international attention. When America's first real contribution to the evolution of the automobile finally came along in 1908, it was far from elegant. Henry Ford's Model T was crude, graceless and virtually devoid of civilizing amenities, but it put personal motorized transport within reach of everyday people for the first time. And changed the world. ● However, even though the Model T spawned plenty of imitators throughout Europe, the imitations had to do with mass production efficiencies, not style. The emergence of anything readily identifiable as an American style came later, and it didn't come from Mr. Ford's shop. By the mid-'20s, a number of manufacturers – Chevrolet in particular – were learning that small but regular changes in size and styling changes that never afflicted the Model T

through 19 years and some 5 million cars) could produce positive sales results. And in 1929, the low-slung Ruxton and its L-29 Cord attracted the attention of automotive designers worldwide. ● The quality that finally allowed for the emergence of a uniquely American design idiom

Previous pages: left, detail of 1939 Packard Darrin convertible; center, top, 1982 Oldsmobile Curved Dash; center, bottom, 1936 Duesenberg Boattail Speedster SJ; right, detail, 1955 Ford Thunderbird. Above, from left to right, 1931 Chrysler Imperial; 1934 Chrysler Airflow; 1958 Oldsmobile Rocket Fastback Coupe; 1963 Chevrolet Corvette Split Window Coupe; At right, detail, 1959 Ford. At left, detail of 1963 Corvette.

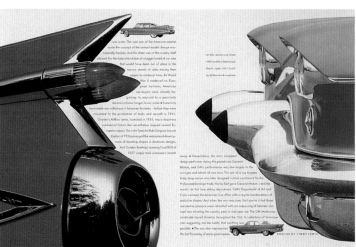

was scale. The vast size of the American market made the concept of the annual model change economically feasible. And the sheer size of the country itself allowed for the natural evolution of a bigger breed of car, one that would have been out of place in the narrow streets of older cities, tracing their origins to medieval times. As World War II coalesced on Euro-pean horizons, American car-buyers were already beginning to respond to a peculiarly American Home Tunger, Laszer, wider ● Some truly memorable cars rolled out of American factories – before they were converted to the production of tanks and aircraft in 1941. Chrysler's Airflow series, launched in 1934, was a disastrous commercial failure that nevertheless inspired several European copies. The John Tjaarda/Bob Gregorie Lincoln Zephyr of 1936 presaged the widespread development of teardrop shapes in American designs. And Gordon Buehrig's stunning Cord 810 of 1937 simply took everyone's breath

At left, details used above, 1959 Cadillac Fleetwood; Detail, right, 1937 Cadillac V-16 Derham Brougham.

away. ● Nevertheless, the most consistent design performer during this period was General Motors, and GM's performance was due largely to the energies and talent of one man. The size of Los Angeles body shops never who later designed custom coachwork for the Hollywood carriage trade, Harley Earl gave General Motors – and the world – its first true styling department. GM's Department of Art and Color nurtured the American love affair with a regular bombardment of seductive shapes. And when the war was over, Earl saw to it that those automotive passions were rekindled with an outpouring of futuristic concept cars traveling the country year in and year out. The GM Motorama caravans toured America throughout the '50s in collections of tomorrow cars suggesting, not too subtly, that anything was possible. ● These also represented the last flowering of some great names.

PHOTOS BY CINDY LEWIS

Detail, far left, 1935 Pierce-Arrow Silver Arrow. Above, from left to right, 1938 Phantom Corsair; Pierce-Arrow; Pierce-Arrow; Detail, far right, 1936 Cord 812.

in American automotive design, Virgil Exner, a graduate of Raymond Loewy and Associates, penned the last truly distinctive designs ever to find their way out of Chrysler Corporation factories, while Loewy himself took credit for the elegant 1953 Studebaker Starlight Coupe. However, "Dutch" Darrin did his best to help save Packard from oblivion with his Clipper series of Clippers, and Bill Mitchell succeeded Harley Earl at General Motors and made Earl's work look stodgy by contrast. ● The 1950s – this period of betterment, believed automotive baroque – is arguably the high-water mark of the American automobile, when American cars were most stylistically distinct from the cars of anywhere else. Whatever practical criticisms one might level at the cars of the '50s – overweight, ill-handling, thirsty – they were fun, a flamboyant expression of an age of innocence. Tony Swan is the automotive editor of Popular Mechanics magazine.

PUBLICATION **Almanac**
ART DIRECTOR **Bridget De Socio**
DESIGNER **Bridget De Socio**
PHOTOGRAPHER **Henry Wolf**
PUBLISHER **Almanac**
CATEGORY **Story Presentation**
DATE **July 1988**

80

PUBLICATION **Almanac**
ART DIRECTOR **Bridget De Socio**
DESIGNER **Bridget De Socio**
ILLUSTRATOR **Raymond Loewy**
PHOTOGRAPHER **Jean Pierre Blusson**
PUBLISHER **Almanac**
CATEGORY **Story Presentation**
DATE **July 1988**

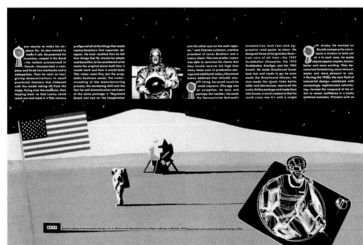

PUBLICATION **LA Style**
DESIGN DIRECTOR **Michael Brock**
DESIGNER **Michael Brock**
PHOTOGRAPHER **Various**
PHOTO EDITOR **Jodi Nakatsuka**
PUBLISHER **LA Style**
CATEGORY **Story Presentation**
DATE **November 1988**

PUBLICATION **Almanac**
ART DIRECTOR **Bridget De Socio**
DESIGNER **Bridget De Socio**
ILLUSTRATOR **Raymond Loewy**
PHOTOGRAPHER **Greg Campbell**
PHOTO EDITOR **Diane Kobar**
PUBLISHER **Almanac**
CATEGORY **Story Presentation**
DATE **July 1988**

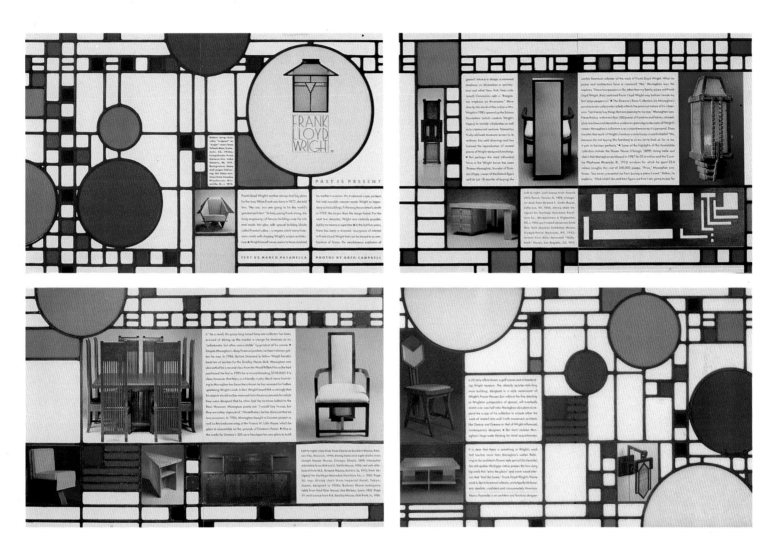

TRUE STORIES

What happens when you take the fantasy out of fashion?
Something magically real.

Photography by GEOF KERN

PUBLICATION **Texas Monthly**
ART DIRECTOR **D.J. Stout**
DESIGNER **D.J. Stout**
PHOTOGRAPHER **Geof Kern**
PUBLISHER **Texas Monthly**
CATEGORY **Story Presentation**
DATE **December 1988**

84

PUBLICATION **Details**
ART DIRECTOR **Lesley Vinson**
DESIGNER **Greg Bergeron, Debbie Smith**
PHOTOGRAPHER **Josef Astor**
PUBLISHER **Advance Publishing Corporation**
CATEGORY **Story Presentation**
DATE **November 1988**

THE ENGLISH TRADITIONALIST

The Romantic

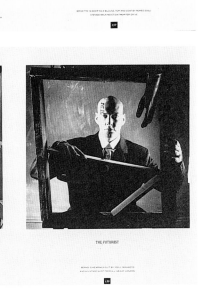

The Existentialist

THE FUTURIST

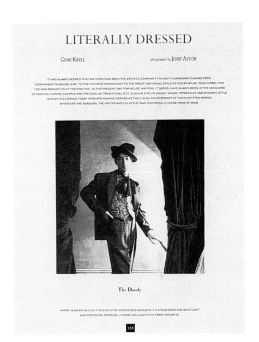

LITERALLY DRESSED

GENE KRELL   *photographed by* JOSEF ASTOR

IT HAS ALWAYS SEEMED THAT WRITERS HAVE BEEN THE ARTISTIC COMMUNITY'S MOST FLAMBOYANT CHARACTERS. FROM BYRON TO BAUDELAIRE TO THE FUTURIST MAYAKOVSKY TO THE GREAT INDIVIDUAL STYLE OF OSCAR WILDE, ROLE MODEL FOR THE NEW ROMANTICS OF THE EIGHTIES. TO THE PRESENT DAY TOM WOLFE, WRITERS, IT SEEMS, HAVE ALWAYS BEEN IN THE VANGUARD OF FASHION. A PRIME EXAMPLE ARE THE ENGLISH TRADITIONALISTS, SUCH AS EVELYN WAUGH, WHOSE IMPRESSIVE AND DYNAMIC STYLE IS MUCH IN EVIDENCE TODAY. PERHAPS FASHION SERVED AS THE VISUAL COUNTERPART OF THEIR WRITTEN WORDS. WHATEVER THE REASONS, THE WRITER AND HIS STYLE HAVE HISTORICALLY GONE HAND IN HAND.

The Dandy

HARRY IS WEARING A SUIT AND SHIRT BY COMME DES GARÇONS, A VINTAGE BROCADE WAISTCOAT AND FEDORA BY MATSUDA. VINTAGE WALKING STICK FROM FOR DRIVE.

85

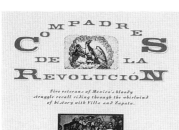

COMPADRES DE LA REVOLUCIÓN

Five veterans of Mexico's bloody struggle recall riding through the whirlwind of history with Villa and Zapata.

BY JAN REID

PHOTOGRAPHY BY DENNIS DARLING

LEO REYNOSA

JESUS GONZALEZ

RAFAEL LORENZANA

MIGUEL CONTRERAS

AUSENCIO R. ARIAS

PUBLICATION **Texas Monthly**
ART DIRECTOR **D.J. Stout**
DESIGNER **D.J. Stout**
PHOTOGRAPHER **Dennis Darling**
PUBLISHER **Texas Monthly**
CATEGORY **Story Presentation**
DATE **November 1988**

PUBLICATION **Texas Monthly**
ART DIRECTOR **D.J. Stout**
DESIGNER **D.J. Stout**
PHOTOGRAPHER **Geof Kern**
PUBLISHER **Texas Monthly**
CATEGORY **Story Presentation**
DATE **September 1988**

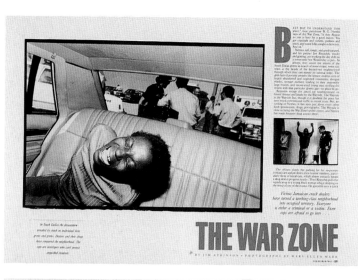

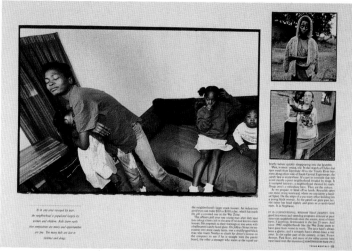

THE WAR ZONE

BY JIM ATKINSON • PHOTOGRAPHS BY MARY ELLEN MARK

Vicious Jamaican crack dealers have turned a working-class neighborhood into occupied territory. Everyone is either a criminal or a victim. Even cops are afraid to go into . . .

PUBLICATION **Texas Monthly**
ART DIRECTOR **D.J. Stout**
DESIGNER **D.J. Stout**
PHOTOGRAPHER **Mary Ellen Mark**
PUBLISHER **Texas Monthly**
CATEGORY **Story Presentation**
DATE **November 1988**

PUBLICATION **Travel & Leisure**
ART DIRECTOR **Bob Ciano**
DESIGNER **Bob Ciano**
PHOTOGRAPHER **John Loengard**
PUBLISHER **American Express**
CATEGORY **Story Presentation**
DATE **April 1988**

HERE'S TO DUBLIN

A BLACK-
AND-WHITE
PORTRAIT OF A
THOUSAND-
YEAR-OLD CITY
BY DAVID HANLY

PHOTOGRAPHED
BY JOHN LOENGARD

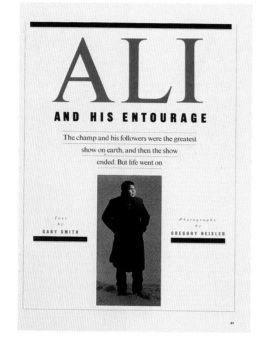

ALI

AND HIS ENTOURAGE

The champ and his followers were the greatest
show on earth, and then the show
ended. But life went on

*Text
by
GARY SMITH*

*Photographs
by
GREGORY HEISLER*

MUHAMMAD ALI

FERDIE PACHECO

LUIS SARRIA

PUBLICATION **Sports Illustrated**
ART DIRECTOR **Steven Hoffman**
DESIGNER **Steven Hoffman/Peter Herbert**
PHOTOGRAPHER **Gregory Heisler**
PUBLISHER **Time, Inc.**
CATEGORY **Story Presentation**
DATE **April 1988**

PUBLICATION **Warfield's**
ART DIRECTOR **Claude Skelton**
DESIGNER **Claude Skelton**
PHOTOGRAPHER **Barry Holniker**
PUBLISHER **The Daily Record**
CATEGORY **Story Presentation**
DATE **September 1988**

THE MOST BEAUTIFUL WOMEN IN L.A.

PUBLICATION **LA Style**
DESIGN DIRECTOR **Michael Brock**
ART DIRECTOR **Marylin Babcock**
DESIGNER **Michael Brock**
PHOTOGRAPHER **Sylvia Plachy**
PHOTO EDITOR **Jodi Nakatsuka**
PUBLISHER **LA Style**
CATEGORY **Story Presentation**
DATE **September 1988**

PUBLICATION **Metropolis**
ART DIRECTOR **Helene Silverman**
DESIGNER **Helene Silverman**
PUBLISHER **Bellerophon Publications**
CATEGORY **Story Presentation**
DATE **July/August 1988**

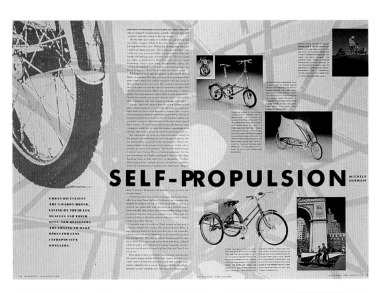

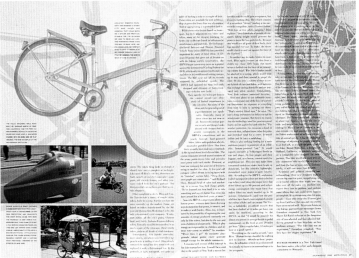

PUBLICATION **Metropolis**
ART DIRECTOR **Helene Silverman**
DESIGNER **Helene Silverman, Jeff Christensen**
PUBLISHER **Bellerophon Publications**
CATEGORY **Story Presentation**
DATE **December 1988**

PUBLICATION **New York**
ART DIRECTOR **Robert best**
PUBLISHER **News Group America**
CATEGORY **Story Presentation**
DATE **October 31, 1988**

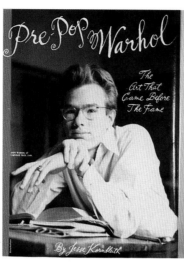

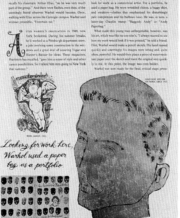

PUBLICATION **Spy**
ART DIRECTOR **B.W. Honeycutt**
DESIGNER **Scott Frommere**
PUBLISHER **Spy Publishing Partners**
CATEGORY **Single Page/Spread**
DATE **December 1988**

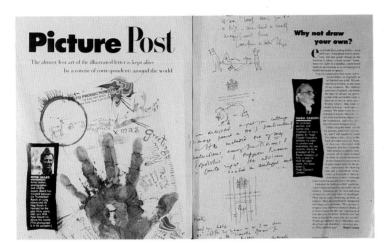

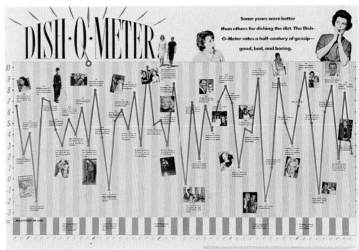

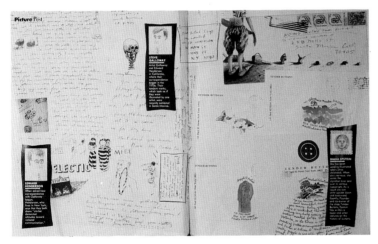

PUBLICATION **HG**
ART DIRECTOR **Karen Grant**
DESIGNER **Derek Ungless**
PUBLISHER **Condé Nast Publications, Inc.**
CATEGORY **Story Presentation**
DATE **May 1988**

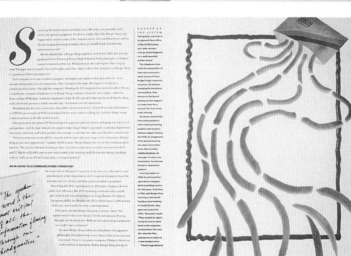

PUBLICATION **Access**
ART DIRECTOR **Bryan Peterson**
DESIGNER **Bryan Peterson**
PHOTOGRAPHER **John Saxon**
CLIENT **Northern Telecom**
AGENCY **Peterson & Company, Dallas, TX**
CATEGORY **Single Page/Spread**
DATE **Winter 1988**

96

PUBLICATION **Mercedes Magazine**
ART DIRECTOR **John Tom Cohoe**
DESIGNER **John Tom Cohoe**
ILLUSTRATOR **Andy Warhol**
CLIENT **Mercedes-Benz of North America**
AGENCY **McCaffrey & McCall, NYC**
CATEGORY **Story Presentation**
DATE **August 1988**

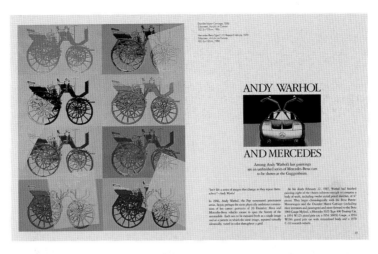

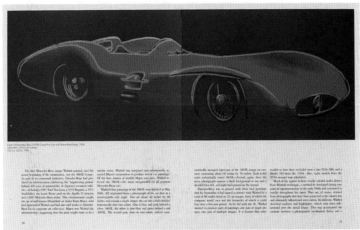

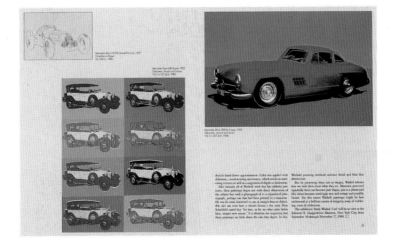

PUBLICATION **Access**
ART DIRECTOR **Bryan Peterson**
DESIGNER **Bryan Peterson**
PHOTOGRAPHER **Robb Debenport**
CLIENT **Northern Telecom**
AGENCY **Peterson & Company, Dallas, TX**
CATEGORY **Single Page/Spread**
DATE **Winter 1988**

98

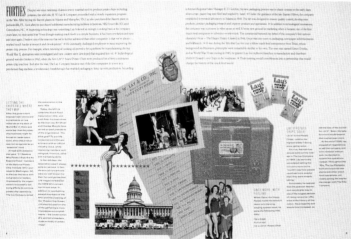

PUBLICATION **Bandwagon**
ART DIRECTOR **Jan Wilson**
DESIGNER **Jan Wilson**
PHOTOGRAPHER **Neill Whitlock**
AGENCY **Peterson & Company, Dallas, TX**
PUBLISHER **Frito-Lay, Inc.**
CATEGORY **Story Presentation**
DATE **Fall 1988**

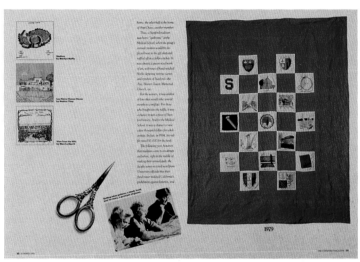

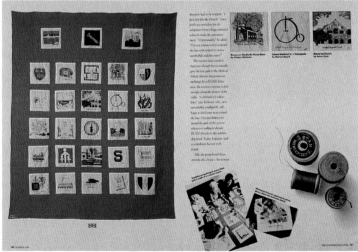

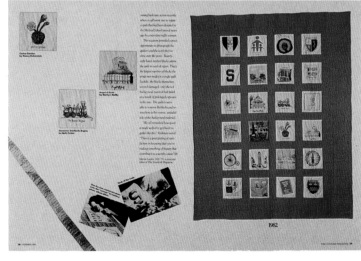

PUBLICATION **The Stanford Magazine**
ART DIRECTOR **Andrew Danish**
DESIGNER **Andrew Danish**
PHOTOGRAPHER **Lee Fatherree, Monica Lee**
PUBLISHER **Stanford Alumni Association**
CATEGORY **Story Presentation**
DATE **Summer 1988**

PUBLICATION **Progressive Architecture**
ART DIRECTOR **Richelle Huff**
DESIGNER **Richelle Huff**
PUBLISHER **Penton Publishing**
CATEGORY **Story Presentation**
DATE **September 1988**

THE DUFFY DESIGN GROUP

FOR THE LAST SEVERAL DECADES, GRAPHIC DESIGN HAS HAD ITS HEROES, THOSE WE HAVE LOOKED UP TO AS THE STANDARD BEARERS, THE BEST OF THE BEST. AND, IN A SENSE, THEY WERE SACROSANCT. HOWEVER, IN RECENT YEARS THE INDUSTRY HAS FOLLOWED THE TREND OF POPULAR CULTURE BY CREATING VIRTUAL "POP STARS"

PUBLICATION **Graphis**
ART DIRECTOR **B. Martin Pedersen**
DESIGNER **B. Martin Pedersen**
PUBLISHER **Graphis Publishing Corporation**
CATEGORY **Story Presentation**
DATE **December 1988**

PUBLICATION **ID**
DESIGN DIRECTOR **Fulton + Partners**
ART DIRECTOR **Gregory Mastrianni**
PUBLISHER **Design Publications, Inc.**
CATEGORY **Story Presentation**
DATE **May/June 1988**

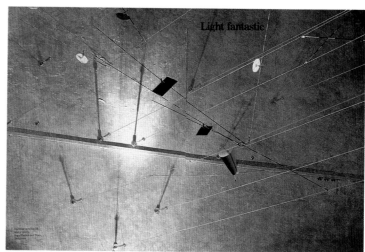

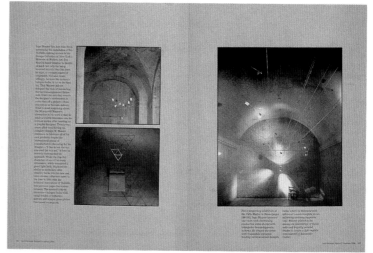

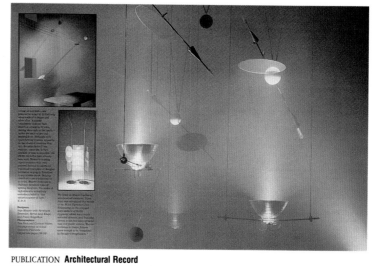

PUBLICATION **Architectural Record**
DESIGN DIRECTOR **Alberto Bucchianeri**
DESIGNER **Anna-Egger Schlesinger**
PUBLISHER **McGraw-Hill**
CATEGORY **Story Presentation**
DATE **September 1988**

PUBLICATION **Progressive Architecture**
ART DIRECTOR **Richelle Huff**
DESIGNER **Richelle Huff**
PUBLISHER **Penton Publishing**
CATEGORY **Story Presentation**
DATE **April 1988**

Pristine Intervention

Charged with the restoration and reconfiguration of a 17th-Century palazzo, architect Guido Canali imposes a cool and delicate installation to expand the National Gallery of Parma.

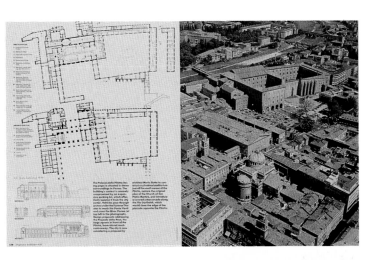

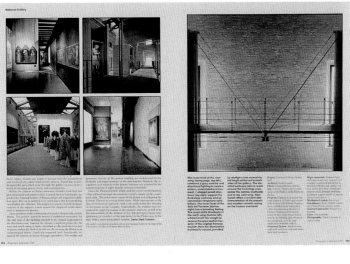

SALUTE

to eight at the
top of the arts —
and their observations
on the obstacles,
past and present

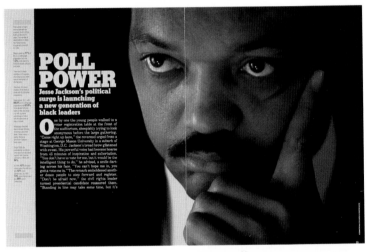

POLL POWER

Jesse Jackson's political
surge is launching
a new generation of
black leaders

O nly one the young people walked to a
voter registration table at the front of
the auditorium, sheepishly trying to look
anonymous before the large gathering.
"Come right up here," the reverend urged from a
stage at George Mason University in a suburb of
Washington, D.C. Jackson's broad brow glistened
with sweat. His powerful voice had become hoarse
from 45 minutes of inspiration and exhortation.
"You don't have to vote for me, but it would be the
intelligent thing to do," he advised, a smile dart-
ing across his face. "You can't hope me in, you
gotta vote me in." The remark emboldened another dozen people to step forward and register.
"Don't be afraid now," the civil rights leader
turned presidential candidate reassured them.
"Standing in line may take some time, but it's

BY BRIAN LANKER

I n this country, being a woman or
being a black has always meant
living life by someone else's
rules. That someone usually was
male and white. For those Americans who are both female and black,
the burden is doubled. Brian
Lanker's photographic essay (which
will be expanded to a book next year)
celebrate that special minority.
Lanker searched out a distinguished
and, indeed, courageous few who
through their words or deeds ad-
vanced the cause of civil rights for
both groups. The women reveal their
determination to break free from
bigotry and charmness, and their
faith that eventually they would.

For some, sexual equality
is as important
as political equality in

RIGHTING WRONGS

ROSA PARKS 75

SEPTIMA POINSETTE CLARK

PUBLICATION **Life**
DESIGN DIRECTOR **Tom Bentkowski**
ART DIRECTOR **Robin E. Brown**
DESIGNER **Robin E. Brown**
PUBLISHER **Time, Inc.**
CATEGORY **Single Issue**
DATE **Spring 1988**

104

PUBLICATION **Life, 150 Years of Photography**
DESIGN DIRECTOR **Tom Bentkowski**
ART DIRECTOR **Nora Sheehan**
DESIGNER **Nora Sheehan**
PUBLISHER **Time, Inc.**
CATEGORY **Single Issue**
DATE **Fall 1988**

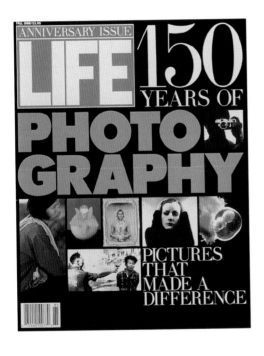

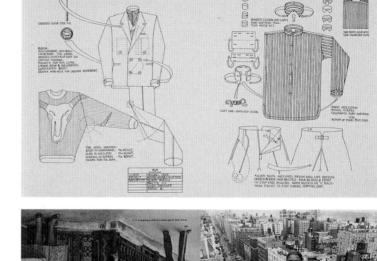

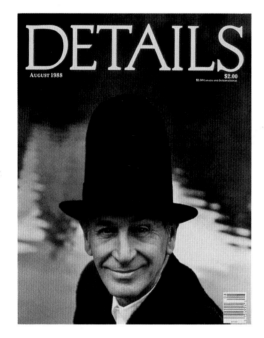

PUBLICATION **Details**
ART DIRECTOR **Lesley Vinson**
DESIGNER **Lesley Vinson, Greg Bergeron, John Hacinli, Debbie Smith**
PHOTOGRAPHER **John Chan, Charoline Olofgors, Pierre-Gilles Vidoli**
PUBLISHER **Advance Publishing Corporation**
CATEGORY **Single Issue**
DATE **August 1988**

PUBLICATION **LA Style**
DESIGN DIRECTOR **Michael Brock**
ART DIRECTOR **Marilyn Babcock**
DESIGNER **Michael Brock, Marilyn Babcock, Gaylen Braun**
PHOTO EDITOR **Jodi Nakatsuka**
PUBLISHER **LA Style**
CATEGORY **Single Issue**
DATE **November 1988**

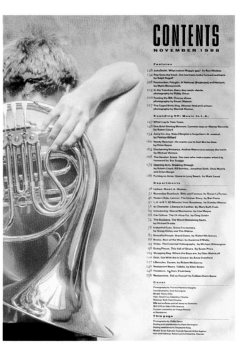

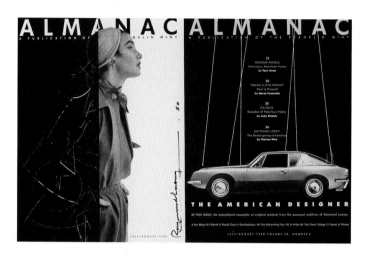

PUBLICATION **Almanac**
ART DIRECTOR **Bridget De Socio**
DESIGNER **Briget De Socio**
ILLUSTRATOR **Raymond Loewy**
PUBLISHER **Almanac**
CATEGORY **Single Issue**
DATE **July 1988**

PUBLICATION **San Francisco Focus**
ART DIRECTOR **Matthew Drace**
DESIGNER **Mark Ulriksen, Hazel Boissiere**
PUBLISHER **KQED, Inc.**
CATEGORY **Single Issue**
DATE **June 1988**

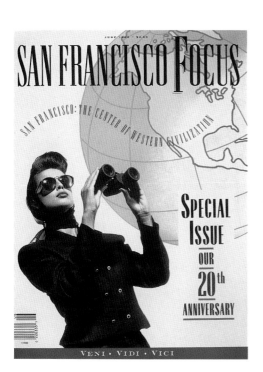

CARLOS ACALA:
They do it against impossible odds. It may seem too people to a fist, but they find their niche.

PUBLICATION **National Geographic**
DESIGN DIRECTOR **Howard E. Paine**
ART DIRECTOR **Constance H. Phelps**
PUBLISHER **National Geographic Society**
CATEGORY **Single Issue**
DATE **February 1988**

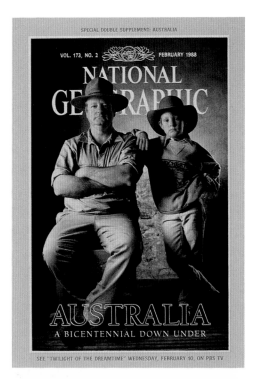

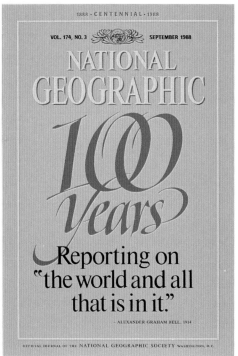

PUBLICATION **National Geographic**
DESIGN DIRECTOR **Howard E. Paine**
PUBLISHER **National Geographic Society**
CATEGORY **Single Issue**
DATE **September 1988**

"Their innocence is as great as Adam's," reported Portuguese explorer Pedro Álvares Cabral of the first Brazilians. Blown too far west on a voyage to India in April 1500, his fleet anchored off an unexpected shore where the people seemed as beautiful as birds. Reports such as his from the New World fostered the idea in Europe of a "noble savage" living in harmony with nature.

In 1986 a hunter named Modigana (right) guided me to his hamlet in the rain forest of Rondônia. His gentle ways belied his reputation for slaying diamond prospectors. He gave me a wristlet of carved beads to increase my strength. Last December he died in the forest, possibly of snakebite. I still wear the wristlet in remembrance of his smile.

"Last Days of Eden"
Rondônia's
Urueu-Wau-Wau
Indians

By LOREN McINTYRE · Photographs by W. JESCO von PUTTKAMER

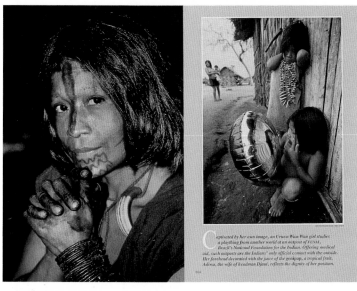

Captivated by her own image, an Urueu-Wau-Wan girl studies a plaything from another world at an outpost of FUNAI, Brazil's National Foundation for the Indian. Offering medical aid, such outposts are the Indians' only official contact with the outside. Her forehead decorated with the juice of the genipap, a tropical fruit, Adiwa, the wife of headman Djaui, reflects the dignity of her position.

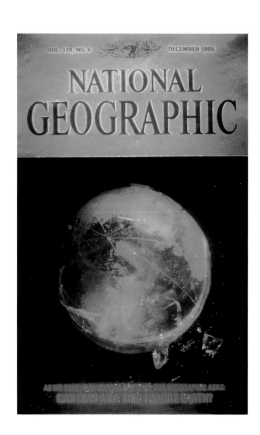

111

PUBLICATION **National Geographic**
DESIGN DIRECTOR **Howard E. Paine**
PUBLISHER **National Geographic Society**
CATEGORY **Single Issue**
DATE **December 1988**

PUBLICATION **Time**
ART DIRECTOR **Rudolph Hoglund, Ina Saltz**
PHOTOGRAPHER **James Nachtwey**
PUBLISHER **Time, Inc.**
CATEGORY **Single Issue**
DATE **December 5, 1988**

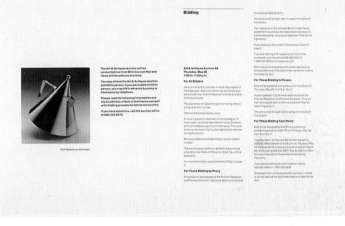

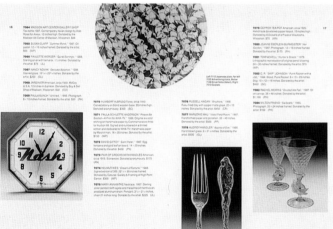

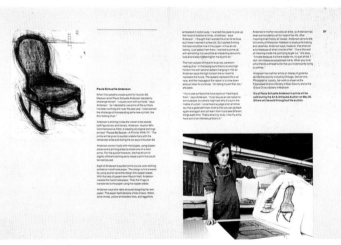

PUBLICATION **Auction '88 Art & Antiques**
ART DIRECTOR **Brian Lorbiecki**
DESIGNER **Brian Lorbiecki**
PHOTOGRAPHER **James Gill**
CLIENT **Friends of WHA-TV**
AGENCY **WHA-TV Design, Madison, WI**
CATEGORY **Single Issue**
DATE **April 1988**

PUBLICATION **Rolling Stone**
ART DIRECTOR **Fred Woodward**
PUBLISHER **Straight Arrow Publishers**
CATEGORY **Single Issue**
DATE **March 24, 1988**

114

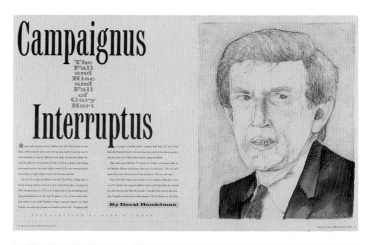

GRACE JONES

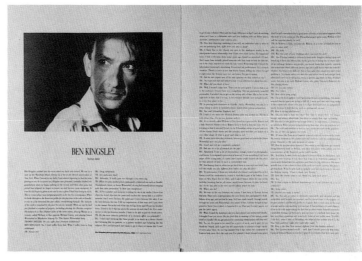

BEN KINGSLEY

PUBLICATION **Splash**
ART DIRECTOR **Jordan Crandall**
DESIGNER **Howell James Gannon, Jr.**
PUBLISHER **Splash Publications, Inc.**
CATEGORY **Single Issue**
DATE **November/December 1988**

PUBLICATION **Art Center Review #3**
ART DIRECTOR **Kit Hinrichs**
DESIGNER **Kit Hinrichs, Karen Boone**
ILLUSTRATOR **Michael Schwab, Doug Boyd**
PHOTOGRAPHER **Steven Heller, Barry Robinson**
CLIENT **Art Center College of Design**
AGENCY **Pentagram Design, San Francisco, CA**
CATEGORY **Single Issue**
DATE **April 1988**

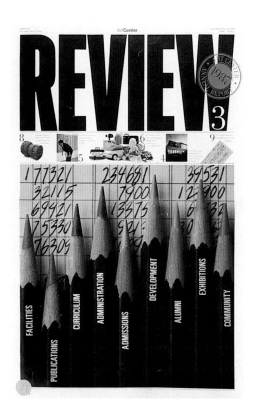

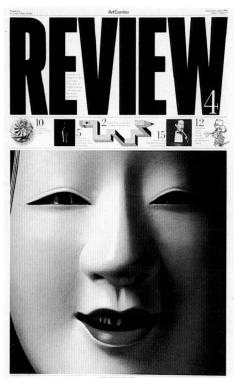

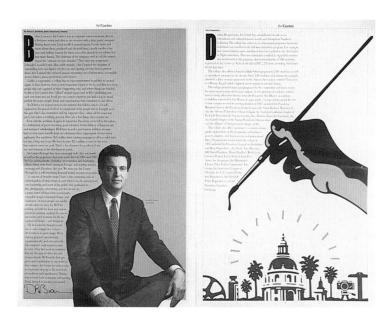

PUBLICATION **Art Center Review #4**
ART DIRECTOR **Kit Hinrichs**
DESIGNER **Kit Hinrichs, Terri Driscoll, Lenore Bartz**
ILLUSTRATOR **John Hersey, Nina Norins, John Cuneo**
PHOTOGRAPHER **Steve Heller, Rick Eskite, Henrik Kam,
Jim Miho, Jim Blakeley, Noritoyo Nakamoto**
PHOTO EDITOR **Art Center College of Design**
CLIENT **Pentagram Design, San Francisco, CA**
PUBLISHER **Single Issue**
CATEGORY **September 1988**

PUBLICATION **Agenda**
DESIGN DIRECTOR **Eric Keller**
ART DIRECTOR **Don Hammond**
ILLUSTRATOR **Michael McGowen**
CLIENT **Chrysler Motor Co.**
AGENCY **The Publications Co.,Detroit, MI**
CATEGORY **Single Issue**
DATE **July 1988**

PUBLICATION **Leaf Annual Report**
ART DIRECTOR **Pat & Greg Samata**
DESIGNER **Pat & Greg Samata**
PHOTOGRAPHER **Mark Joseph, Terry Heffernan**
CLIENT **N.W. Ayer**
AGENCY **Samata Associates, Dundee, IL**
CATEGORY **Single Issue**
DATE **April 1988**

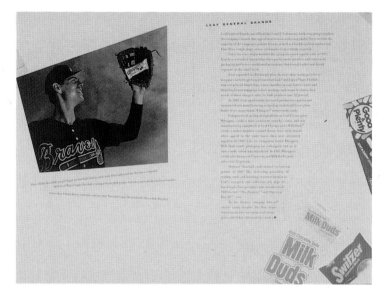

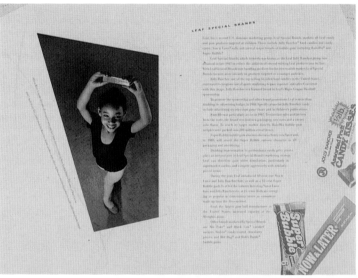

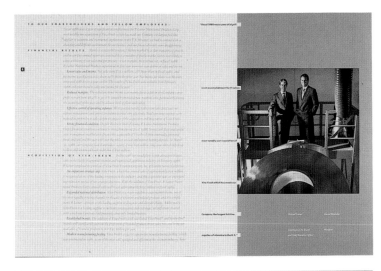

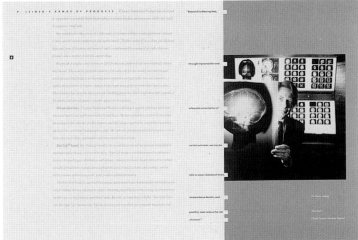

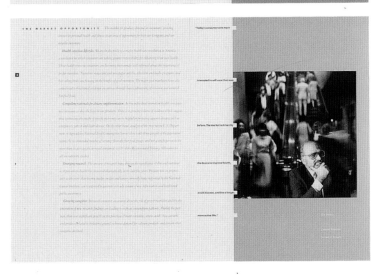

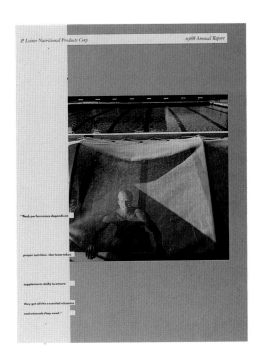

PUBLICATION **P. Leiner Nutritional Products Corp. Annual Report**
DESIGN DIRECTOR **Rik Besser**
ART DIRECTOR **Douglas Joseph**
DESIGNER **Douglas Joseph**
PHOTOGRAPHER **Jeff Corwin**
CLIENT **P.Leiner Nutritional Products Corp.**
AGENCY **Besser Joseph Partners, Santa Monica, CA**
CATEGORY **Single Issue**
DATE **June 1988**

PUBLICATION **Bandwagon**
ART DIRECTOR **Jan Wilson**
DESIGNER **Jan Wilson**
PHOTOGRAPHER **Neill Whitlock**
AGENCY **Peterson & Company, Dallas, TX**
PUBLISHER **Frito-Lay, Inc.**
CATEGORY **Story Presentation**
DATE **Fall 1988**

FIFTIES

While the Un-American Activities Committee investigated people's political beliefs and the U.S. and the U.S.S.R. waged Cold War in Korea, America turned on to hula hoops, Elvis Presley and "I Love Lucy." Drive-in theaters and 3-D glasses were "cool," as were ducktails and leather jackets, poodle skirts and bobby socks. Marilyn Monroe married Joe DiMaggio, Jacqueline Bouvier wed Senator John F. Kennedy and Grace Kelly tied the knot with Prince Rainier of Monaco. Polio crippled thousands of children, bomb shelters multiplied in backyards across the U.S., and the Space Race began when the Soviets launched Sputnik I.

FORTIES

Japan's bombing of Pearl Harbor plunged America into World War II. While thousands of men enlisted in the armed services in the weeks after the attack, women entered the work force in record numbers. Rationing was under way, since all supplies were required for the war effort. Betty Grable's legs inspired the boys overseas, while Greer Garson's "Mrs. Miniver" touched families stateside. In 1945, serving an unprecedented fourth term, President Franklin Delano Roosevelt gave the order to drop the atom bomb on Hiroshima and Nagasaki. The war finally over, soldiers returned home from "Over There." Not surprisingly, the baby boom began.

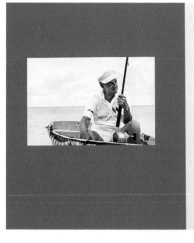

Why It Pays to Go Fishing.

Law is a Whole New Ball Game.

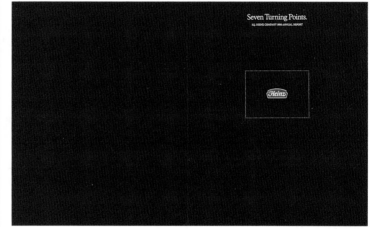

Seven Turning Points.
HJ HEINZ COMPANY 1988 ANNUAL REPORT

Heinz

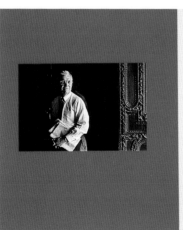

Common Sense Time in the Common Market.

PUBLICATION HJ Heinz Annual Report
ART DIRECTOR Bennett Robinson
DESIGNER Bennett Robinson
PHOTOGRAPHER Rodney Smith
CLIENT HJ Heinz Corporation
AGENCY Corporate Graphics, NYC
CATEGORY Single Issue
DATE December 1988

PUBLICATION **Lockheed Aeronautical Systems Company**
DESIGN DIRECTOR **Rod Dyer**
ART DIRECTOR **Steve Twigger**
DESIGNER **Steve Twigger**
ILLUSTRATOR **Steve Twigger**
CLIENT **Lockheed**
AGENCY **Ward Watanabe Productions, San Francisco, CA**
PUBLISHER **Lockheed Aeronautical**
CATEGORY **Single Issue**
DATE **1988**

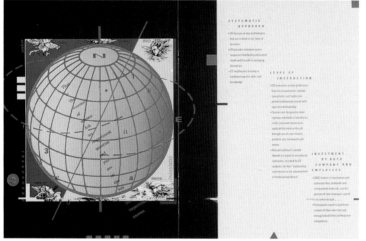

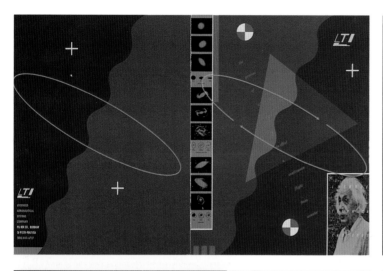

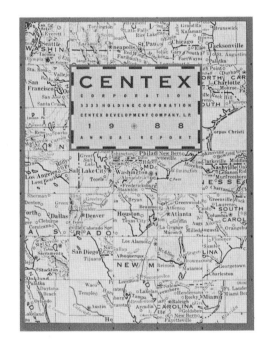

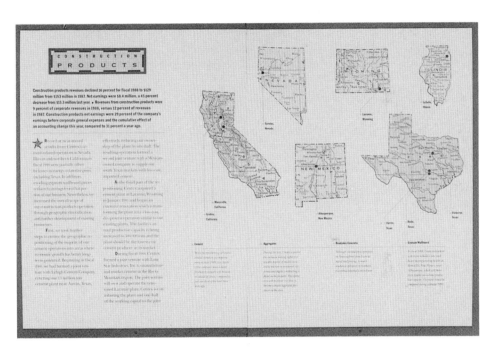

PUBLICATION **Centex Corporation Annual Report**
ART DIRECTOR **Woody Pirtle**
DESIGNER **Woody Pirtle, Alan Colvin**
ILLUSTRATOR **Lana Brown**
PHOTOGRAPHER **Michael Haynes**
CLIENT **Centex Corporation**
AGENCY **Pentagram Design, NYC**
CATEGORY **Single Issue**
DATE **1988**

PUBLICATION **Boston Symphony Annual Report**
DESIGN DIRECTOR **Christopher Passehl**
ART DIRECTOR **William Wondriska**
DESIGNER **Christopher Passehl**
PHOTO EDITOR **Christopher Passehl**
CLIENT **Boston Symphony Orchestra**
AGENCY **Wondriska Associates Inc., Farmington, CT**
CATEGORY **Single Issue**
DATE **May 1988**

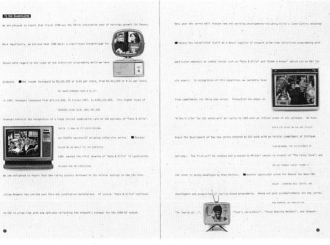

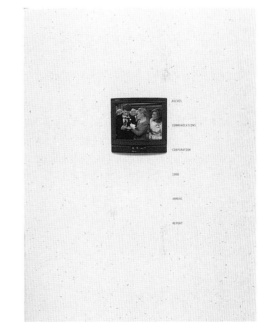

PUBLICATION **Reeves Communication Corporation Annual Report**
ART DIRECTOR **Aubrey Balkind**
DESIGNER **David Suh**
PHOTOGRAPHER **Paul Stevens, Michael Melford**
CLIENT **Reeves Communication Corporation**
AGENCY **Frankfurt, Gips, Balkind, NYC**
CATEGORY **Single Issue**
DATE **December 1988**

PUBLICATION **Time Inc. Annual Report**
ART DIRECTOR **Philip Gips, Kent Hunter**
DESIGNER **Kent Hunter, Jennifer Long**
ILLUSTRATOR **Javier Romero**
PHOTOGRAPHER **Neil Selniek**
CLIENT **Time, Inc.**
AGENCY **Frankfurt, Gips, Balkind, NYC**
CATEGORY **Single Issue**
DATE **March 1988**

126

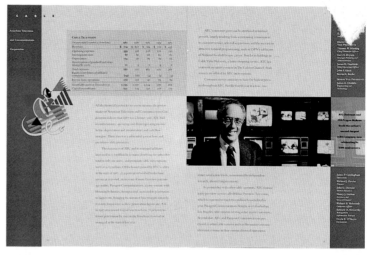

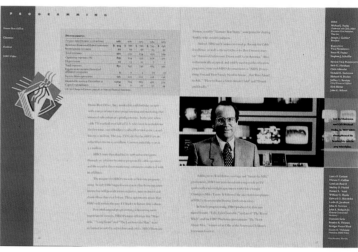

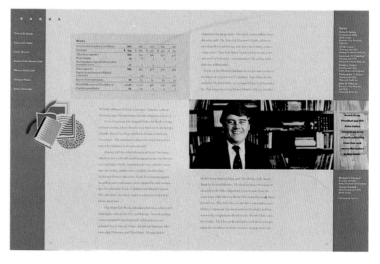

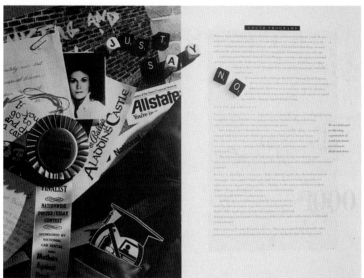

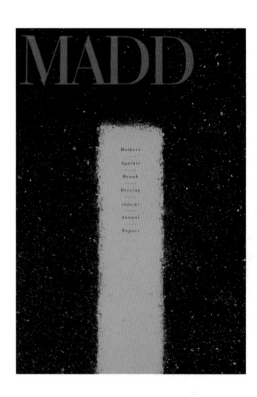

PUBLICATION **MADD Annual Report**
ART DIRECTOR **Bryan Peterson**
DESIGNER **Bryan Peterson**
PHOTOGRAPHER **Paul Talley**
CLIENT **Mothers Against Drunk Driving**
AGENCY **Peterson & Company, Dallas, TX**
CATEGORY **Single Issue**
DATE **March 1988**

PUBLICATION **NME Annual Report**
ART DIRECTOR **Kit Hinrichs**
DESIGNER **Kit Hinrichs, Karen Boone**
ILLUSTRATOR **Vince Perez, Justin Carroll, Tim Lewis**
PHOTOGRAPHER **Michele Clement, Terry Heffernan, Jeff Corwin**
CLIENT **National Medical Enterprises**
AGENCY **Pentagram Design, San Francisco, CA**
CATEGORY **Single Issue**
DATE **August 1988**

128

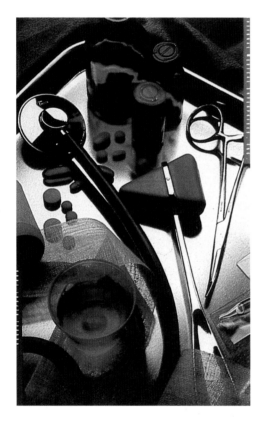

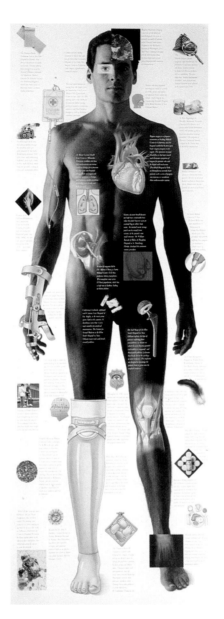

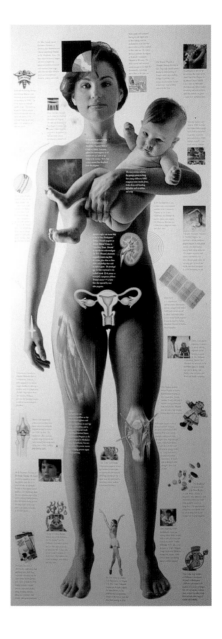

PUBLICATION **Skald**
ART DIRECTOR **Kit Hinrichs**
DESIGNER **Kit Hinrichs, Karen Berndt**
ILLUSTRATOR **Tim Lewis, Dugald Stermer, Mark Summers**
PHOTOGRAPHER **Harvey Lloyd, Barry Robinson**
CLIENT **Royal Viking Line**
AGENCY **Pentagram Design, San Francisco, CA**
CATEGORY **Single Issue**
DATE **Spring 1988**

PUBLICATION **Potlach Corporation Annual**
ART DIRECTOR **Kit Hinrichs**
DESIGNER **Kit Hinrichs, Lenore Bartz**
ILLUSTRATOR **Doug Smith, Mark Summers, Max Seabaugh**
PHOTOGRAPHER **Tom Tracy, Barry Robinson**
CLIENT **Potlach Corporation**
AGENCY **Pentagram Design, San Francisco, CA**
CATEGORY **Single Issue**
DATE **April 1988**

PUBLICATION **George Rice & Sons Electronic Prepress**
ART DIRECTOR **Gary Hinsche**
DESIGNER **Gary Hinsche**
PHOTOGRAPHER **Robert Stevens Photography**
CLIENT **George Rice & Sons Printers & Lithographers**
AGENCY **Robert Miles Runyan & Associates, NYC**
CATEGORY **Single Issue**
DATE **July 1988**

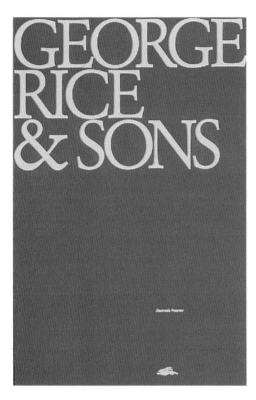

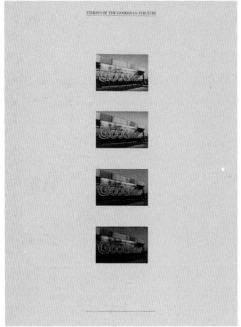

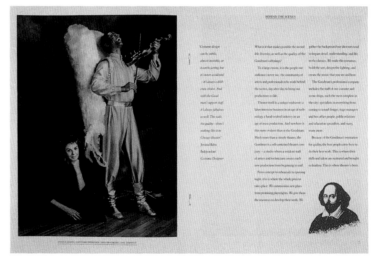

PUBLICATION **Visions of The Goodman Theatre**
ART DIRECTOR **Kym Abrams**
DESIGNER **Kym Abrams**
PHOTOGRAPHER **Eric Hausman**
CLIENT **The Goodman Theatre**
AGENCY **Kym Abrams Design, Chicago, IL**
CATEGORY **Single Issue**
DATE **January/April 1988**

PUBLICATION **Micron Annual Report**
ART DIRECTOR **Linda Svonavec**
DESIGNER **Linda Owens**
PHOTOGRAPHER **Steven Welsh**
CLIENT **Micron Technology, Inc.**
AGENCY **Floathe & Associates, Bellevue, WA**
CATEGORY **Single Issue**
DATE **December 1988**

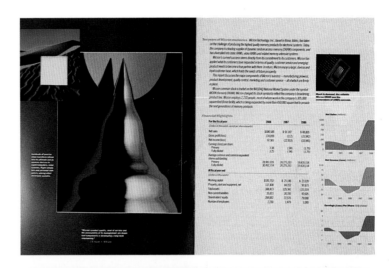

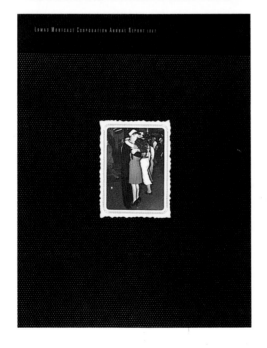

PUBLICATION **Lomas Mortgage Corporation Annual Report**
ART DIRECTOR **Brian Boyd**
DESIGNER **Brian Boyd**
PHOTOGRAPHER **Greg Booth**
CLIENT **Lomas Mortgage Corporation**
AGENCY **The Richards Group, Dallas, TX**
CATEGORY **Single Issue**
DATE **March 1988**

PUBLICATION **Times Mirror Annual Report**
ART DIRECTOR **Jim Berte**
DESIGNER **Jim Berte**
ILLUSTRATOR **Paul Bice**
CLIENT **The Times Mirror Company**
AGENCY **Robert Miles Runyan & Associates, Playa del Rey, CA**
CATEGORY **Single Issue**
DATE **June 1988**

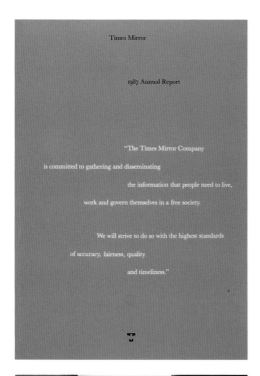

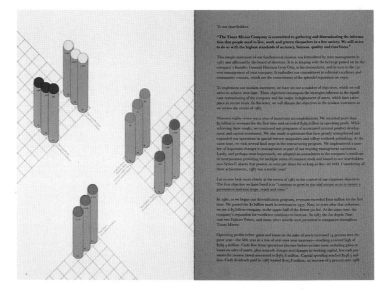

PUBLICATION **UNISYS Performance**
ART DIRECTOR **Eric Madsen**
DESIGNER **Eric Madsen, Tim Sauer**
ILLUSTRATOR **Frank Miller, Mark Herman, Jan-Willem Boer**
PHOTOGRAPHER **Kerry Peterson, Nancy Bundt**
CLIENT **UNISYS Defense Systems Corporation**
AGENCY **Madsen & Kuenster, Minneapolis, MN**
CATEGORY **Single Issue**
DATE **Fall 1988**

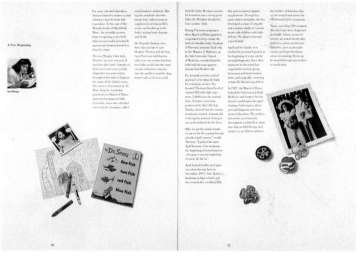

PUBLICATION **March of Dimes/Birth Defects Foundation Annual Report**
ART DIRECTOR **Eugene Grossman**
DESIGNER **Eugene Grossman**
PHOTOGRAPHER **David Sunberg**
CLIENT **March of Dimes/Birth Defects Foundation**
AGENCY **Anspach, Grossman, Portugal, NYC**
CATEGORY **Single Issue**
DATE **August 10, 1988**

PUBLICATION **Computer Sciences Corporation Annual Report**
ART DIRECTOR **Robert Miles Runyan**
DESIGNER **Michael Mescall**
PHOTOGRAPHER **Scott Morgan**
CLIENT **Computer Sciences Corporation**
AGENCY **Robert Miles Runyan & Associates, Playa del Rey, CA**
CATEGORY **Single Issue**
DATE **June 1988**

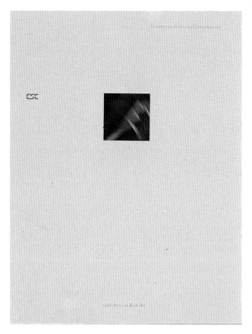

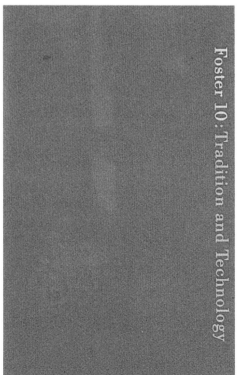

PUBLICATION **Foster 10: Tradition and Technology**
ART DIRECTOR **Robert Miles Runyan**
DESIGNER **Edie Garrett**
CLIENT **Obunsha, Ltd.**
AGENCY **Robert Miles Runyan & Associates, Playa del Rey, CA**
CATEGORY **Single Issue**
DATE **April 1988**

PUBLICATION **University Circle, Inc. Annual Report**
ART DIRECTOR **Joyce Nesnadny**
DESIGNER **Joyce Nesnadny**
PHOTOGRAPHER **Mark Schwartz**
PHOTO EDITOR **Mark Schwartz**
CLIENT **University Circle, Inc.**
AGENCY **Nesnadny & Schwartz, Cleveland, OH**
CATEGORY **Single Issue**
DATE **October 1988**

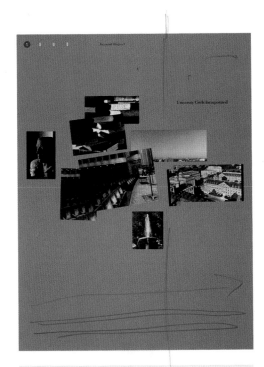

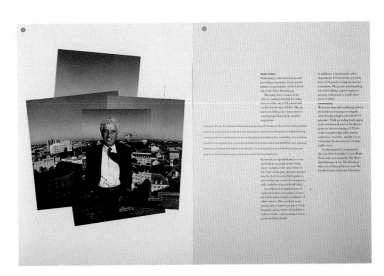

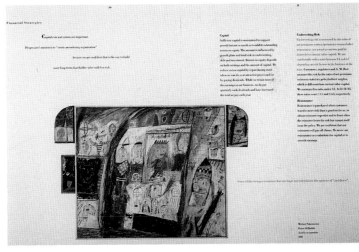

PUBLICATION **The Progressive Corporation Annual Report**
ART DIRECTOR **Joyce Nesnadny**
DESIGNER **Joyce Nesnadny, Richard Stermole**
PHOTOGRAPHER **Stephen Tannock**
CLIENT **The Progressive Corporation**
AGENCY **Nesnadny & Schwartz, Cleveland, OH**
CATEGORY **Single Issue**
DATE **March 1988**

PUBLICATION **MCI World**
ART DIRECTOR **Kin Yuen**
DESIGNER **Kin Yuen**
CLIENT **MCI Communications Corporation, NYC**
AGENCY **Frankfurt Gips Balkind, NYC**
CATEGORY **Single Issue**
DATE **November/December 1988**

■ A secure environment for your records

Your documents are protected by a sophisticated fire and security alarm. Smoke detectors, heat detectors, sprinkler system and intrusion devices provide an extremely secure environment.

The warehouse is monitored 24 hours a day, 7 days a week by a U.L. approved central station

For security purposes, only authorized individuals with a valid password are allowed to request documents. In addition, only Off-Site employees physically handle the documents.

SECURITY . . . .

24 Hrs.

■ Quick access to your information

Access

ACCESS

ACCE S S

Each box is numbered and assigned a short description of the contents. This information is entered into our computer system. Your boxes are tracked by the computer and are

readily available in the event you need quick access to the information

Quarterly inventory reports along with receipts of recent box deposits provide an on going and accurate list of all your inactive boxes.

■ Time savings for your staff

Let us help you and your staff save time. When you need quick and easy access to your boxed records, simply phone us with your box request and we take over from there. Your information is quickly located and retrieved thanks to our computerized operation. We then promptly deliver the box of information to you. In addition, we can fax documents, mail documents or you can view the document at our record center.

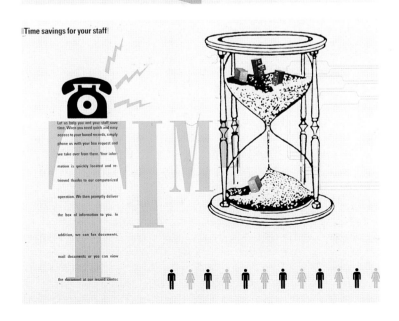

The key to record storage

Off-site

Record Management

PUBLICATION **Off-Site Record Management**
ART DIRECTOR **Earl Gee**
DESIGNER **Earl Gee**
ILLUSTRATOR **Earl Gee**
PHOTOGRAPHER **Bill Delzell**
CLIENT **Off-Site Record Management**
AGENCY **Earl Gee Design, NYC**
CATEGORY **Single Issue**
DATE **November 1988**

PUBLICATION **MMA Bulletin**
DESIGN DIRECTOR **Betty Binns, David Skolkin**
ART DIRECTOR **Joan Holt**
DESIGNER **David Skolkin**
PUBLISHER **Metropolitan Museum of Art**
CATEGORY **Single Issue**
DATE **Spring 1988**

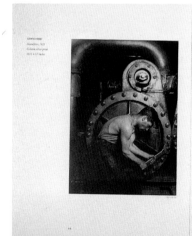

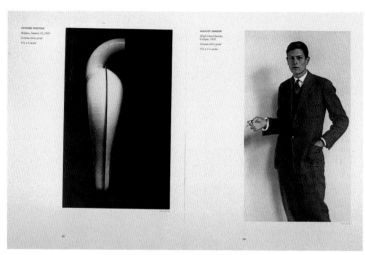

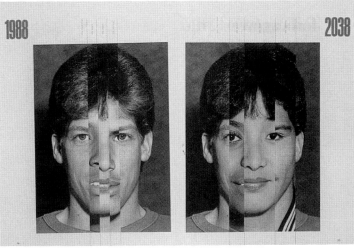

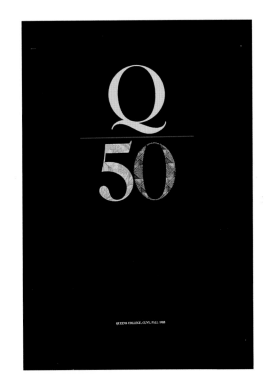

PUBLICATION **Q**
ART DIRECTOR **Milton Glaser**
DESIGNER **Suzanne Zumpano**
PHOTO EDITOR **Nina Suban**
CLIENT **Queens College**
AGENCY **Milton Glaser, Inc., NYC**
CATEGORY **Single Issue**
DATE **May 1988**

PUBLICATION **The Simpson Paper Company**
ART DIRECTOR **Roger Cook, Don Shanosky**
DESIGNER **Roger Cook, Don Shanosky, Robert Frankle**
PHOTOGRAPHER **Carlos Eguiguren**
CLIENT **The Simpson Paper Company**
AGENCY **Cook & Shanosky Associates, Inc., Princeton, NJ**
CATEGORY **Single Issue**
DATE **September 1988**

140

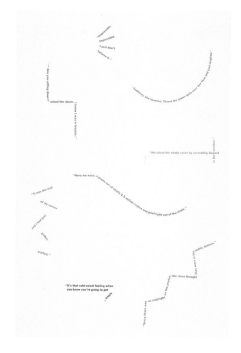

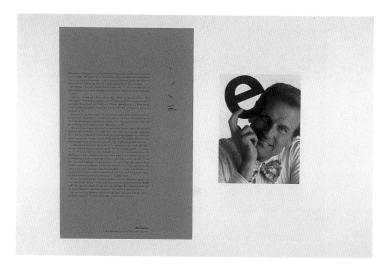

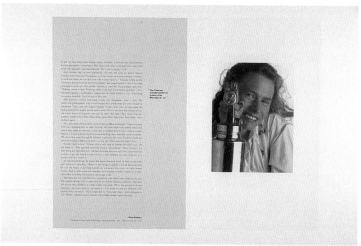

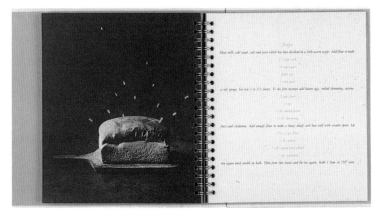

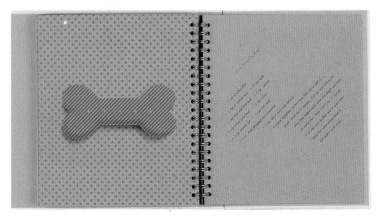

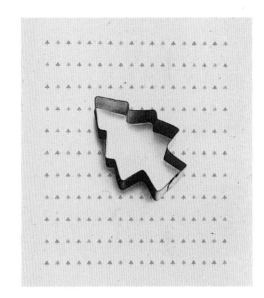

PUBLICATION **Samata Christmas Book**
ART DIRECTOR **Pat & Greg Samata**
DESIGNER **Pat & Greg Samata**
ILLUSTRATOR **Paul Thompson**
AGENCY **Samata Associates, Dundee, IL**
CATEGORY **Single Issue**
DATE **December 1988**

PUBLICATION **Design Quarterly 141**
DESIGN DIRECTOR **Craig Davidson**
ART DIRECTOR **Nancy Skolos**
DESIGNER **Nancy Skolos**
PHOTOGRAPHER **Glen Halverson, Peter Latner**
CLIENT **Walker Art Center**
AGENCY **The Schrafft Center, Charlestown, MA**
CATEGORY **Single Issue**
DATE **Winter 1988**

DQ

I4I

Minneapolis Sculpture Garden

Growing the Garden

Martin Friedman

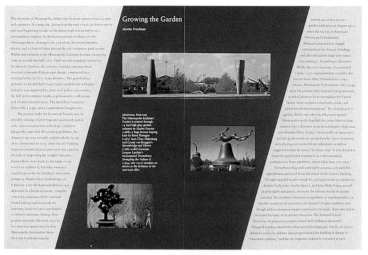

PUBLICATION **Warner Communications**
ART DIRECTOR **Peter Harrison, Harold Burch**
DESIGNER **Harold Burch, Peter Harrison**
ILLUSTRATOR **John Van Hammersveld**
PHOTOGRAPHER **Scott Morgan**
CLIENT **Warner Communications, Inc.**
AGENCY **Pentagram Design, NYC**
CATEGORY **Single Issue**
DATE **March 1988**

PUBLICATION **Warner Communications**
ART DIRECTOR **Peter Harrison, Harold Burch**
DESIGNER **Harold Burch, Christina Freyss**
ILLUSTRATOR **Harold Burch, David Suter, Tim Lewis, Jerry Ordway, Chris Wozniak**
PHOTOGRAPHER **Scott Morgan**
CLIENT **Warner Communications, Inc.**
AGENCY **Pentagram Design, NYC**
CATEGORY **Single Issue**
DATE **December 1988**

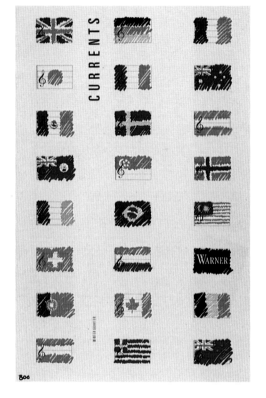

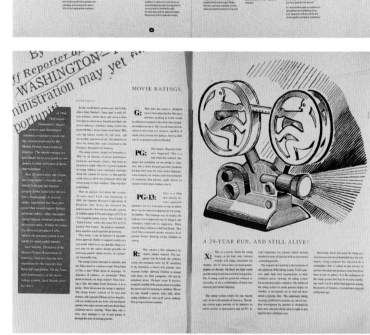

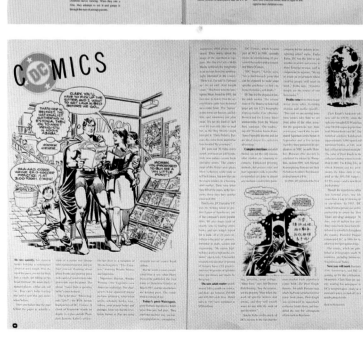

PUBLICATION **Warner Communications**
ART DIRECTOR **Peter Harrison, Harold Burch**
DESIGNER **Harold Burch**
ILLUSTRATOR **Neil Shigley, Javier Romero, David Suter**
PHOTOGRAPHER **Scott Morgan, Jack Freed, Bill Whitehurst**
CLIENT **Warner Communications, Inc.**
AGENCY **Pentagram Design, NYC**
CATEGORY **Single Issue**
DATE **October 1988**

PUBLICATION **Zoo Views**
ART DIRECTOR **Ken Cook**
DESIGNER **Ken Cook**
PHOTOGRAPHER **Steven Underwood, John Blaustein**
CLIENT **San Francisco Zoo**
AGENCY **Cross Associates, San Francisco, CA**
CATEGORY **Single Issue**
DATE **September/October 1988**

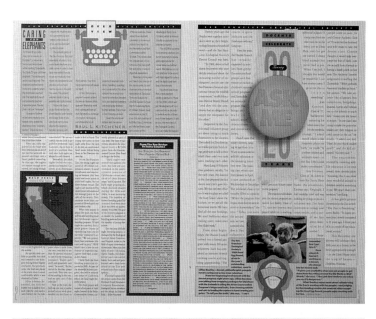

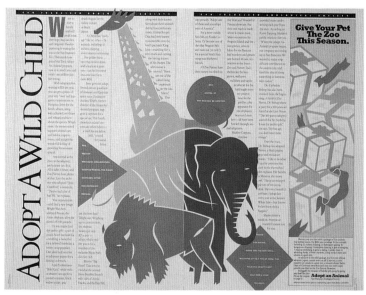

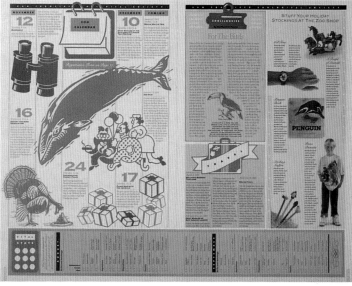

PUBLICATION **Zoo Views #2**
ART DIRECTOR **Ken Cook**
DESIGNER **Ken Cook**
PHOTOGRAPHER **Steven Underwood, John Blaustein**
CLIENT **San Francisco Zoo**
AGENCY **Cross Associates, San Francisco, CA**
CATEGORY **Single Issue**
DATE **November/December 1988**

PUBLICATION **Progressive Architecture**
ART DIRECTOR **Richelle Huff**
DESIGNER **Richelle Huff**
PUBLISHER **Penton Publishing**
CATEGORY **Single Issue**
DATE **September 1988**

148

P/A Profile
Kuramata Design Office, Tokyo

Issey Miyake Men boutique, Minami-Aoyama, Tokyo, 1987

This two-story shop has a main stair of embossed aluminum enhancanced by a secondary stair of painted steel (facing page). Clothes hang from steel cables, on the lower level (facing page, top level) display shelves are made of glass rods.

Shiro Kuramata.

Breaking the Bonds

Designer Shiro Kuramata's quest for weightlessness turns prosaic materials into poetic essays on the nature of the ephemeral.

P/A Profile
Jed Johnson & Alan Wanzenberg

Apartment, New York

P/A Profile
Kuramata Design Office

Issey Miyake Men boutique, Shibuya Seibu Department Store, Tokyo, 1987

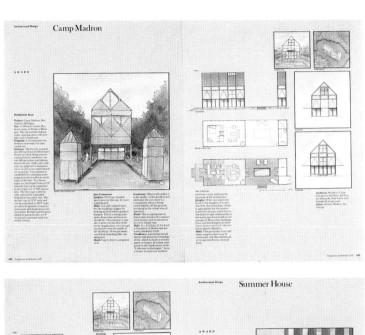

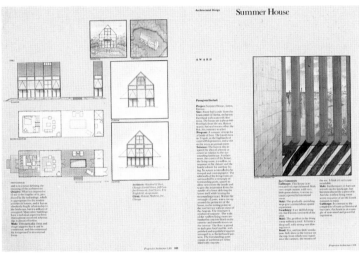

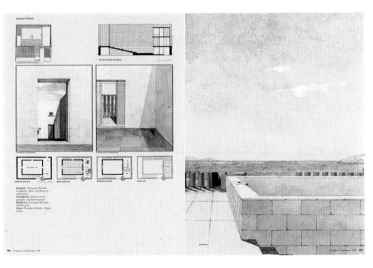

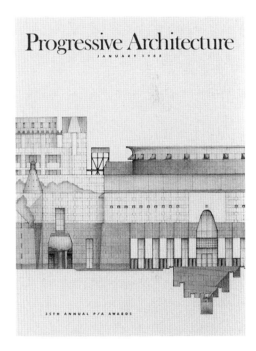

PUBLICATION **Progressive Architecture**
ART DIRECTOR **Richelle Huff**
DESIGNER **Richelle Huff**
PUBLISHER **Penton Publishing**
CATEGORY **Single Issue**
DATE **January 1988**

PUBLICATION **Graphis**
ART DIRECTOR **B. Martin Pedersen**
DESIGNER **B. Martin Pedersen**
PUBLISHER **Graphis Publishing Corporation**
CATEGORY **Single Issue**
DATE **April 1988**

150

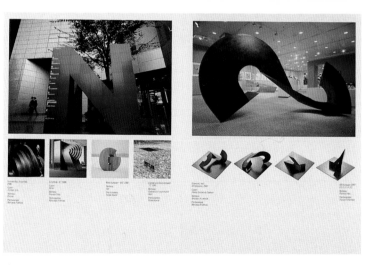

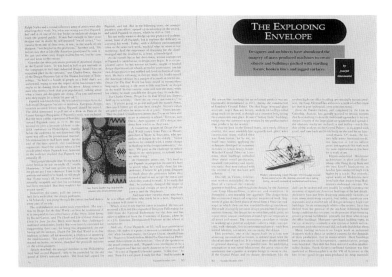

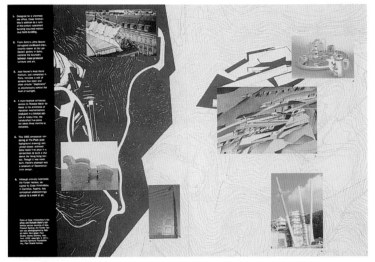

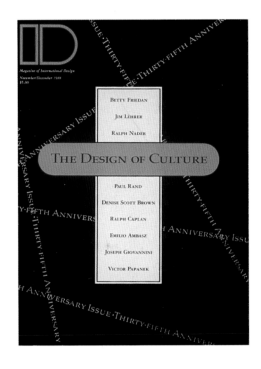

PUBLICATION **ID**
DESIGN DIRECTOR **Fulton + Partners**
ART DIRECTOR **Gregory Mastrianni**
PUBLISHER **Design Publications, Inc.**
CATEGORY **Single Issue**
DATE **November/December 1988**

PUBLICATION **Computer System News**
DESIGN DIRECTOR **Joe McNeill**
ART DIRECTOR **Nicole White**
PHOTOGRAPHER **Danuta Otfinowski**
PUBLISHER **CMP Publications**
CATEGORY **Single Issue**
DATE **November 1988**

EDWARD TELLER
Nuclear Physicist

JOHN IMLAY
Management Science of America CEO

JAMES BIRKENSTOCK
IBM Executive

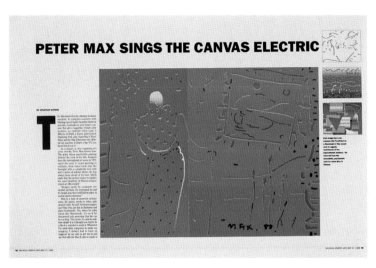

PETER MAX SINGS THE CANVAS ELECTRIC

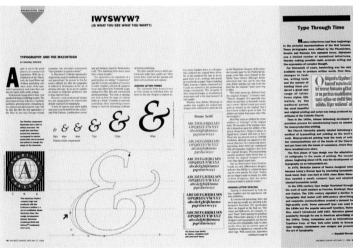

IWYSWYW?
(IS WHAT YOU SEE WHAT YOU WANT?)

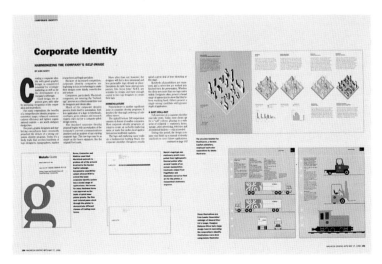

Corporate Identity

GA
MacWEEK's Graphic Arts Supplement

Maximizing the Mac Style

Macintosh Art by Peter Max

153

PUBLICATION **MacWeek**
ART DIRECTOR **Eleanor Leishman**
PUBLISHER **MacWeek**
CATEGORY **Single Issue**
DATE **May 1988**

PUBLICATION **Life**
ART DIRECTOR **Tom Bentkowski**
DESIGNER **Ellen Kostroff**
PUBLISHER **Time, Inc.**
CATEGORY **Special Section**
DATE **May 1988**

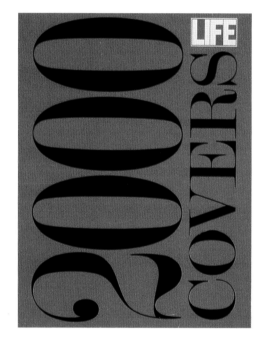

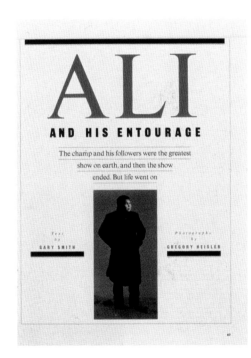

PUBLICATION **Sports Illustrated**
ART DIRECTOR **Steven Hoffman**
DESIGNER **Steven Hoffman, Peter Herbert**
PHOTOGRAPHER **Gregory Heisler**
PUBLISHER **Time, Inc.**
CATEGORY **Special Section**
DATE **April 25, 1988**

PUBLICATION **Motor**
ART DIRECTOR **Harold A. Perry**
DESIGNER **Harold A. Perry, Joe Anderson**
ILLUSTRATOR **Russell von Sauers**
PHOTOGRAPHER **Jim Richards**
PUBLISHER **The Hearst Corporation**
CATEGORY **Special Section**
DATE **December 1988**

EXPERT TRAINING GUIDE

MOTOR MAGAZINE

ETG

EMISSION CONTROL HARDWARE

By Norman Mayersohn

Illustrations Russell von Sauers

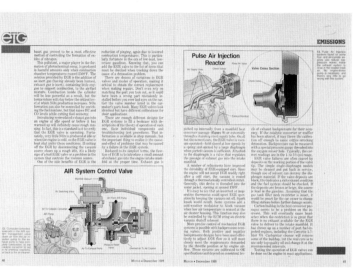

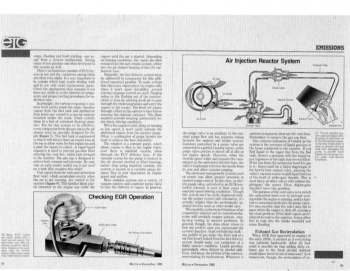

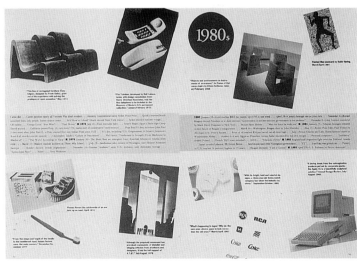

For thirty-five years *ID* has showcased the milestones and masterpieces of design, along with a fair share of its mistakes. And so to astonish, amuse, delight and inspire, we offer, interspersed throughout this special anniversary issue, a kaleidoscopic view of *ID*'s memorable projects, a **timeline of design.**

1950s

1970s

1960s

1980s

PUBLICATION **ID**
ART DIRECTOR **Gregory Mastrianni**
DESIGNER **Gregory Mastrianni**
PUBLISHER **Design Publications, Inc.**
CATEGORY **Special Section**
DATE **November/December 1988**

PUBLICATION **Financial Times of Canada**
ART DIRECTOR **Therese Shechter**
DESIGNER **Therese Shechter, Gary Hall**
PHOTOGRAPHER **Paul Lawrence**
PUBLISHER **Financial Times of Canada**
CATEGORY **Special Section**
DATE **November 14, 1988**

158

PUBLICATION **The Washington Times**
ART DIRECTOR **Joseph Scopin**
DESIGNER **Dolores Motichka, Paul Woodward**
PUBLISHER **The Washington Times**
CATEGORY **Special Section**
DATE **November 1988**

PUBLICATION **The Washington Times**
ART DIRECTOR **Joseph Scopin**
PHOTOGRAPHER **Carol T. Powers**
PUBLISHER **The Washington Times**
CATEGORY **Special Section**
DATE **April 1, 1988**

160

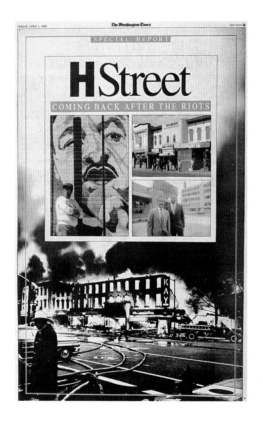

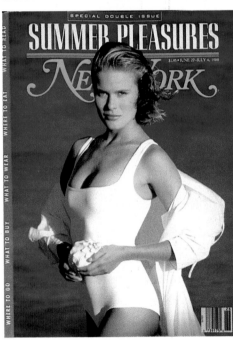

PUBLICATION **New York**
ART DIRECTOR **Robert Best**
PUBLISHER **News Group America**
CATEGORY **Overall**
DATE **April 4, 1988**

PUBLICATION **Rolling Stone**
ART DIRECTOR **Fred Woodward**
PUBLISHER **Straight Arrow Publishers**
CATEGORY **Overall**
DATE **December 15, 1988**

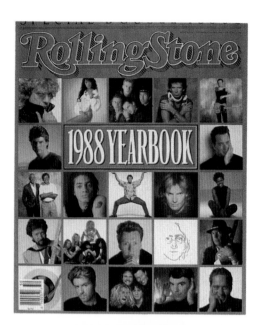

BROOKE SHIELDS

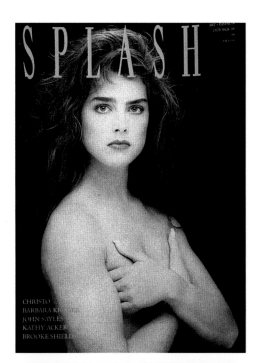

ISABELLA ROSSELLINI

PUBLICATION **Splash**
ART DIRECTOR **Jordan Crandall**
DESIGNER **Howell James Gannon, Jr.**
PUBLISHER **Splash Publications, Inc.**
CATEGORY **Overall**
DATE **November/December 1988**

PUBLICATION **Almanac**
ART DIRECTOR **Bridget De Socio**
DESIGNER **Bridget De Socio**
PHOTOGRAPHER **Mark Lyon**
PUBLISHER **Almanac**
CATEGORY **Overall**
DATE **January 1988**

164

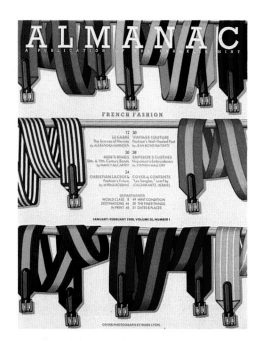

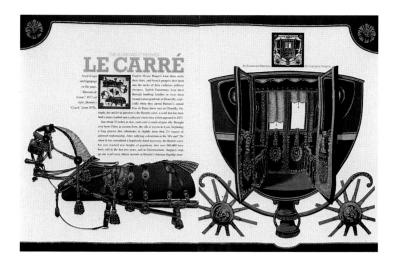

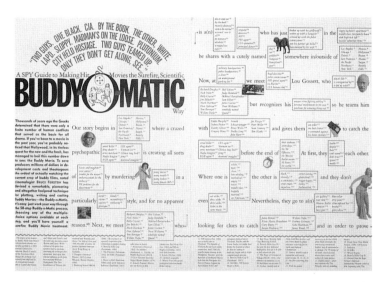

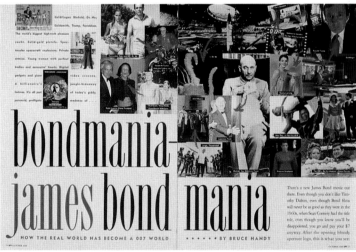

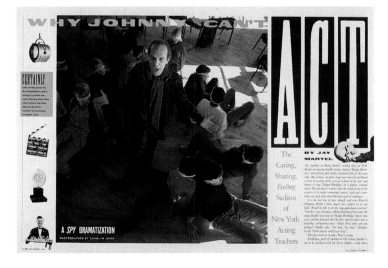

PUBLICATION **Spy**
ART DIRECTOR **B. W. Honeycutt**
DESIGNER **Alexander Knowlton, Scott Frommer,**
Michael Hofmann
PUBLISHER **Spy Publishing Partners**
CATEGORY **Overall**

PUBLICATION **Vanity Fair**
ART DIRECTOR **Charles Churchward**
DESIGNER **Charles Churchward**
PHOTO EDITOR **Elisabeth Biondi**
PUBLISHER **Condé Nast Publications, Inc.**
CATEGORY **Overall**
DATE **March 1988**

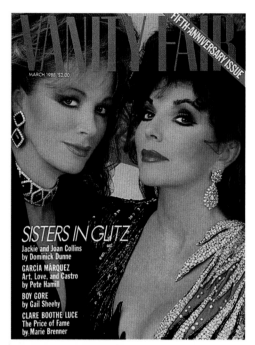

166

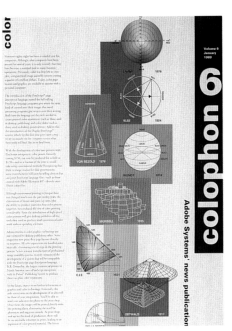

PUBLICATION **Colophon 6**
ART DIRECTOR **Russell Brown**
DESIGNER **Laurie Szujewska**
CLIENT **Adobe Systems, Inc.**
CATEGORY **Overall**
DATE **December 1988**

PUBLICATION **V**
ART DIRECTOR **Terry R. Koppel**
DESIGNER **Terry R. Koppel**
PUBLISHER **Fairfield Publications**
CATEGORY **Overall**
DATE **September 1988**

168

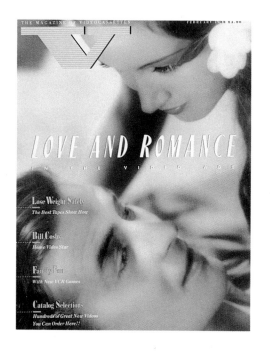

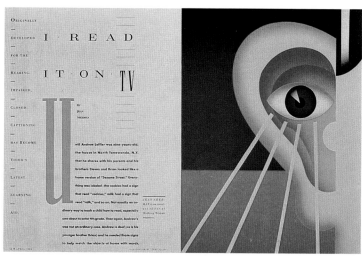

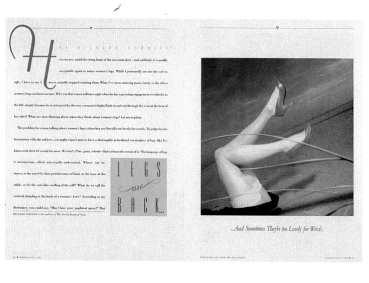

...And Sometimes They're too Lovely for Words.

The global economy demands a

Strategic
new business strategy for the 1990s.

Alliances

By Philip J. Kazzaz

Chairman Lord Blakenham Pearson

Competitiveness, not protectionism

1992 and
is the goal, says a leading member of

International

the European Commission.

Trade

by Willy De Clerq

169

PUBLICATION **Viewpoint**
ART DIRECTOR **Peter Deutsch, Tia Adler**
CLIENT **Ernst & Whitney International**
AGENCY **Deutsch Design, Inc., NYC**
CATEGORY **Overall**
DATE **November 1988**

PUBLICATION **Graphis**
ART DIRECTOR **B. Martin Pedersen**
DESIGNER **B. Martin Pedersen**
PHOTOGRAPHER **Sandi Fellman**
PUBLISHER **Graphis Publishing Corporation**
CATEGORY **Overall**
DATE **February 1988**

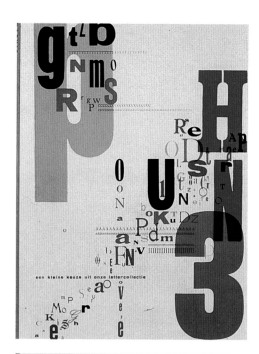

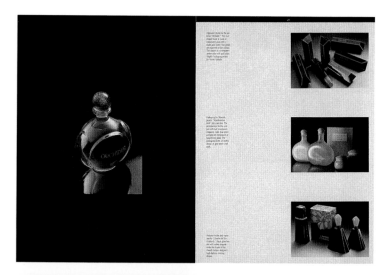

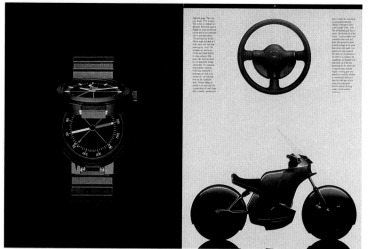

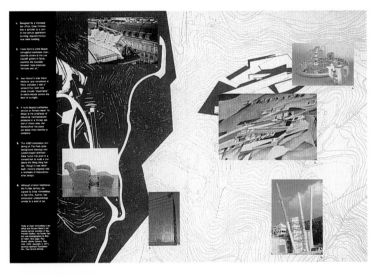

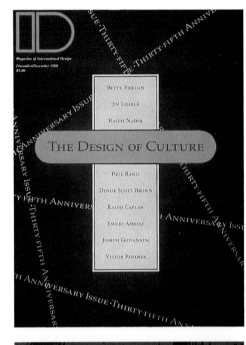

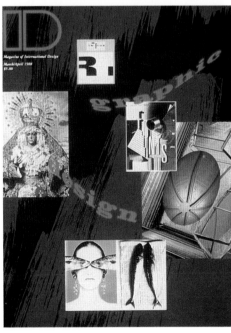

PUBLICATION **ID Magazine**
ART DIRECTOR **Gregory Mastrianni**
DESIGNER **Gregory Mastrianni**
PUBLISHER **Design Publications**
CATEGORY **Overall**
DATE **November/December 1988**

PUBLICATION **Governing**
ART DIRECTOR **Peggy Robertson**
PUBLISHER **Time Publishing Company**
CATEGORY **Overall**
DATE **December 1988**

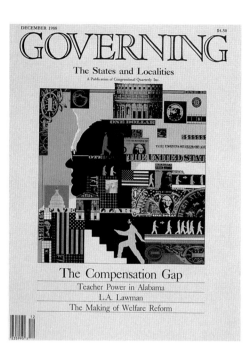

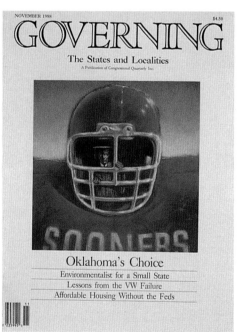

172

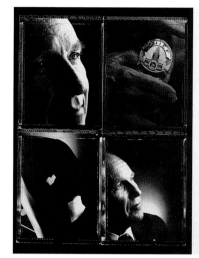

SILK GLOVE STEEL FIST

THE TROPOSCATTER LINK

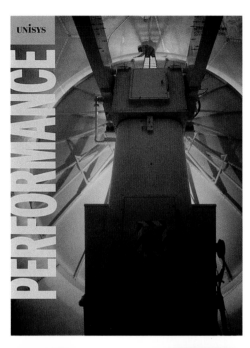

173

PUBLICATION **UNYSIS Performance**
ART DIRECTOR **Eric Madsen**
DESIGNER **Eric Madsen, Tim Sauer**
CLIENT **UNYSIS Corporation Defense Systems**
AGENCY **Madsen & Kuester, Minneapolis, MN**
CATEGORY **Overall**
DATE **1988**

PUBLICATION **The Washington Times**
ART DIRECTOR **William Castronuovo, John Kascht**
DESIGNER **Paul Watts**
ILLUSTRATOR **John Kascht**
PUBLISHER **The Washington Times**
CATEGORY **Overall**
DATE **November 22, 1988**

174

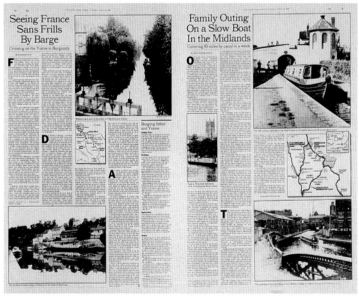

PUBLICATION **The New York Times Travel Section**
ART DIRECTOR **Michael Valenti**
DESIGNER **Michael Valenti**
PUBLISHER **The New York Times**
CATEGORY **Overall**
DATE **April 10, 1988**

PUBLICATION **Tennessee Illustrated**
ART DIRECTOR **Mary Workman**
DESIGNER **Mary Workman**
PUBLISHER **Whittle Communications**
CATEGORY **New Magazine**
DATE **May / June 1988**

176

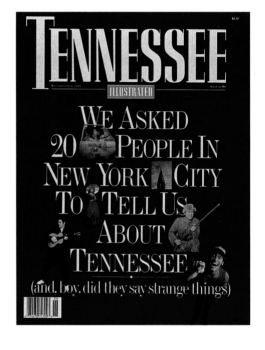

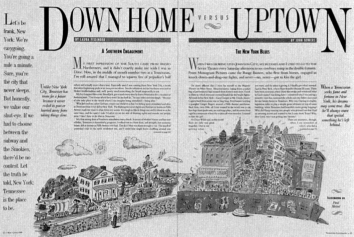

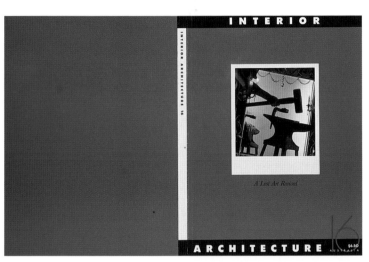

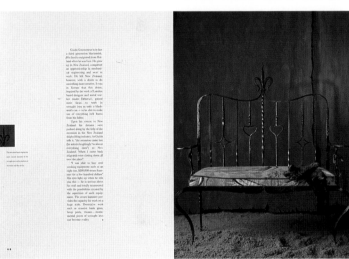

PUBLICATION **Interior Architecture**
ART DIRECTOR **Natalie Bowra**
DESIGNER **Natalie Bowra**
PHOTOGRAPHER **Ashley Barber**
PUBLISHER **YPMA Publications**
CATEGORY **New Magazine**
DATE **December 1988**

PUBLICATION **V**
ART DIRECTOR **Terry R. Koppel**
DESIGNER **Terry R. Koppel**
ILLUSTRATOR **Rico Lins**
PHOTOGRAPHER **Marcos Santili**
PUBLISHER **Fairfield Publications**
CATEGORY **New Magazine**
DATE **February 1988**

178

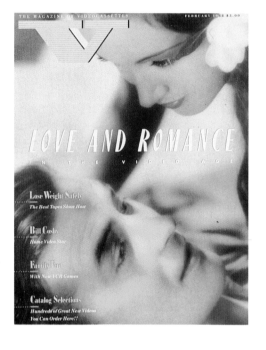

managing

GROWTH

A
GOOD
BUSINESS
PLAN
IS
A
PLAN
OF
ACTION

by timothy j. hickey

by daryl l. mark

CAREER CHANGE
how to cope

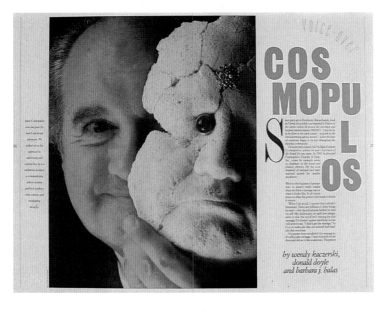

COS MOPU L S OS

by wendy kaczerski, donald doyle and barbara j. balas

DIRECTION
Creative Club of Boston

The theme of this premiere issue "On Your Own"—dedicated to the creative professional who works for a living

WELCOME
to the revolution

by george gendron

179

PUBLICATION **Direction**
DESIGN DIRECTOR **Ronn Campisi**
ART DIRECTOR **Ronn Campisi**
CLIENT **Creative Club of Boston**
AGENCY **Ronn Campisi Design, Boston, MA**
CATEGORY **New Magazine**
DATE **Spring 1988**

PUBLICATION **American Museum of the Moving Image**
ART DIRECTOR **Jane Kosstrin, David Sterling**
DESIGNER **David Slatoff**
PHOTOGRAPHER **Victor Schraeger**
CLIENT **American Museum of the Moving Image**
AGENCY **DoubleSpace, NYC**
CATEGORY **New Magazine**
DATE **September 1988**

180

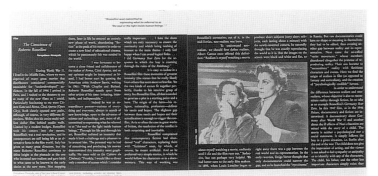

PUBLICATION **Annandale**
DESIGN DIRECTOR **Jane Kosstrin, David Sterling**
DESIGNER **David Slatoff**
PHOTOGRAPHER **Esther Kiviat**
CLIENT **Bard College**
AGENCY **DoubleSpace, NYC**
CATEGORY **New Magazine**
DATE **Fall 1988**

PUBLICATION **Almanac**
ART DIRECTOR **Bridget De Socio**
DESIGNER **Bridget De Socio**
PHOTOGRAPHER **Mark Lyon**
PUBLISHER **Almanac**
CATEGORY **Redesign**
DATE **March/April 1988**

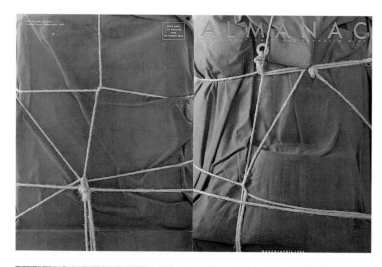

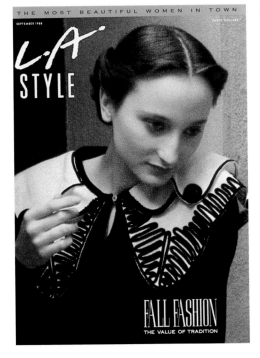

183

PUBLICATION **LA Style**
DESIGN DIRECTOR **Michael Brock**
ART DIRECTOR **Marylin Babcock**
DESIGNER **Michael Brock, Marylin Babcock, Gaylen Braun**
PHOTO EDITOR **Jodi Nakatsuka**
PUBLISHER **LA Style**
CATEGORY **Redesign**
DATE **September 1988**

PUBLICATION **HG**
ART DIRECTOR **Karen Grant**
DESIGNER **Derek Ungless**
PUBLISHER **Condé Nast Publications, Inc.**
CATEGORY **Redesign**
DATE **March 1988**

184

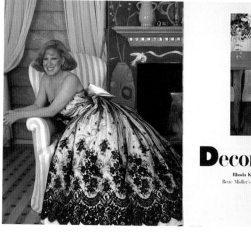

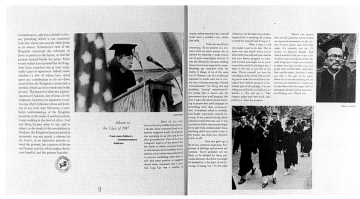

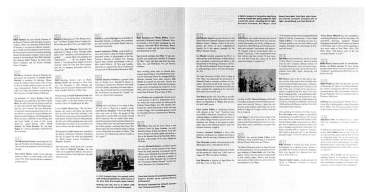

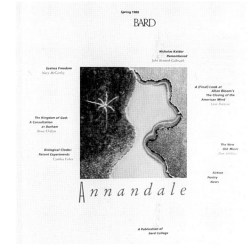

PUBLICATION **Annandale**
ART DIRECTOR **Dan Schillaci**
CLIENT **Bard College**
AGENCY **Doublespace**
PUBCATEGORY **Redesign**
DATE **Spring 1988**

PUBLICATION **Yellow in Motion**
DESIGN DIRECTOR **John Muller**
ART DIRECTOR **Patrice Eilts**
DESIGNER **Patrice Eilts**
ILLUSTRATOR **Tom Patrick**
PHOTOGRAPHER **Mike Regnier**
PHOTO EDITOR **Partice Eilts**
CLIENT **Yellow Freight Systems**
AGENCY **Muller & Co., Kansas City, MO**
CATEGORY **Redesign**
DATE **1988**

186

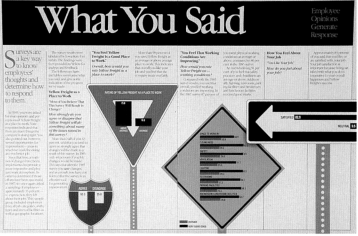

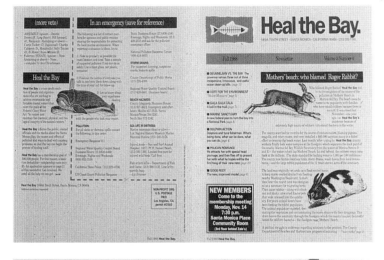

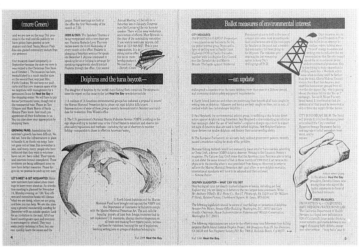

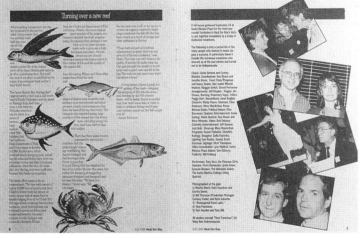

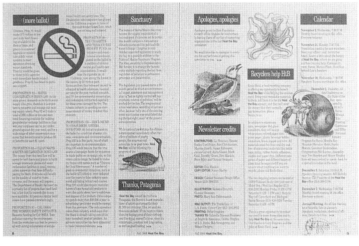

PUBLICATION **Heal the Bay Newsletter**
ART DIRECTOR **Gunnar Swanson**
DESIGNER **Gunnar Swanson**
ILLUSTRATOR **Gunnar Swanson**
PHOTOGRAPHER **Mary Ann Dolcemascold**
CLIENT **Heal the Bay**
AGENCY **Gunnar Swanson Design Office, Venice, CA**
CATEGORY **Redesign**
DATE **Fall 1988**

PUBLICATION **VLSI System Designs**
ART DIRECTOR **Terry V. Koppel**
DESIGNER **Terry V. Koppel**
PUBLISHER **CMP Publications**
CATEGORY **Redesign**
DATE **June 1988**

EIGHT DOLLARS • A CMP PUBLICATION • JUNE 1988

VLSI Systems Design
FOR DESIGNERS OF HIGH-PERFORMANCE SYSTEMS

SOME RISC CHIPS ARE BORN PERFORMERS

EIGHT DOLLARS • A CMP PUBLICATION • JULY 1988

VLSI Systems Design
FOR DESIGNERS OF HIGH-PERFORMANCE SYSTEMS

ASIC FOUNDRIES: KEY PLAYERS IN CREATING YOUR SYSTEM

Structures

RISC
Changes the BALANCE

The quest for speed has driven microprocessor architectures

BOB CUSHMAN, SENIOR EDITOR

Tools

BEHAVIORAL
DESCRIPTIONS IN
V·H·D·L

DAVID J. BARTON, INTERMETRICS INC., BETHESDA, MD.

Methods

Writing
Your Own
CAE Tools

MARTY DEKHAM, TEKTRONIX INC., CAE INSTRUMENTS DIVISION, BEAVERTON, ORE.

PUBLICATION **VPM - Veterinary Practice Mgt.**
DESIGN DIRECTOR **Bett McLean**
ART DIRECTOR **Deb Hardison, Lawrence Woodhull**
DESIGNER **Deb Hardison, Lawrence Woodhull**
PHOTO EDITOR **Sara Elder**
PUBLISHER **Whittle Communications**
CATEGORY **Redesign**
DATE **1988**

PUBLICATION **Financial Times of Canada**
ART DIRECTOR **Therese Shechter**
DESIGNER **Therese Shechter, Gary Hall**
PUBLISHER **Financial Times of Canada**
CATEGORY **Redesign**
DATE **December 5, 1988**

190

PUBLICATION **The Guardian**
ART DIRECTOR **David Hillman**
DESIGNER **David Hillman, Leigh Brownsword**
PUBLISHER **The Guardian**
CATEGORY **Redesign**
DATE **December 2, 1988**

PUBLICATION **Wisconsin State Journal**
DESIGN DIRECTOR **Kenneth Miller, Robert Lockwood**
ART DIRECTOR **Kenneth Miller**
PUBLISHER **Wisconsin State Journal**
CATEGORY **Redesign**
DATE **November 13, 1988**

WISCONSIN STATE JOURNAL

NASA weaves tangled web in shuttle's wake

The drought ends for Bucky

Arafat calls for U.S. shift in Mideast

Dedication keeps UW's Morton going

Businesses laboring in Baby Bust

SPORTS

They got what they deserved

Defense does it all for UW

Scores twice, saves game

Michigan rolls into Rose Bowl

Wisconsin lands Milwaukee's McGee

Bucks top hobbling Celtics

UW skaters sweep past Sioux

METRO

Mistakes cost GOP Senate bid

Conviction ends murder retrial

A ride the hard way

Briton: Waldheim lied

Klein-Dickert cleared of bias, retaliation

State lottery link planned

State delegation will miss Proxmire's clout

OUTLOOK

CHALLENGER: What really happened?

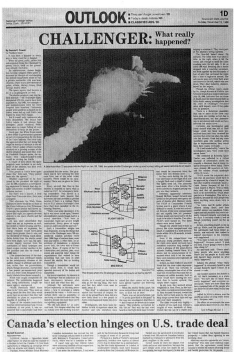

Canada's election hinges on U.S. trade deal

MONEY

Dairy Expo pays off for Wisconsin firms

Led by genetics, export sales are increasing

CUNA Mutual gets fit, ensuring healthy profit

'Tremendous year' follows the slump of '87

If I were you, Mr. Bush, here's what I'd do ...

SHOWCASE

Art of survival

Artist beats the odds

20 years of making learning fun

Holiday Art Fair

ILLUStration

PUBLICATION **Manner Vogue**
ART DIRECTOR **Beda Acherman**
ILLUSTRATOR **Brian Cronin**
PUBLISHER **Condé Nast Publications, Inc.**
CATEGORY **Single Page/Spread**
DATE **December 1988**

194

PUBLICATION **Details**
ART DIRECTOR **Lesley Vinson**
DESIGNER **Lesley Vinson**
ILLUSTRATOR **Isabelle Dervaux**
PUBLISHER **Advance Publishing Corporation**
CATEGORY **Cover**
DATE **March 1988**

PUBLICATION **The Plain Dealer**
ART DIRECTOR **Gerald Sealy**
DESIGNER **Gerald Sealy**
ILLUSTRATOR **Rob Day**
PUBLISHER **Cleveland Plain Dealer**
CATEGORY **Cover**
DATE **October 23, 1988**

PUBLICATION **The Washington Post Magazine**
ART DIRECTOR **Brian Noyes**
DESIGNER **Brian Noyes**
ILLUSTRATOR **Brad Holland**
PUBLISHER **The Washington Post**
CATEGORY **Cover**
DATE **August 14, 1988**

PUBLICATION **Rolling Stone**
ART DIRECTOR **Fred Woodward**
DESIGNER **Fred Woodward**
ILLUSTRATOR **Paul Davis**
PUBLISHER **Straight Arrow Publishers**
CATEGORY **Single Page/Spread**
DATE **April 7, 1988**

PUBLICATION **Regardies**
ART DIRECTOR **John Korpics**
DESIGNER **John Korpics**
ILLUSTRATOR **Matt Mahurin**
PUBLISHER **Regardies, Inc.**
CATEGORY **Single Page/Spread**
DATE **November 1988**

PUBLICATION **Omni**
ART DIRECTOR **Dwayne Flinchum**
DESIGNER **Rani Levy**
ILLUSTRATOR **Brad Holland**
PUBLISHER **Omni Publications International**
CATEGORY **Single Page/Spread**
DATE **December 1988**

PUBLICATION **The Atlantic Monthly**
ART DIRECTOR **Judy Garlan**
DESIGNER **Judy Garlan**
ILLUSTRATOR **Brad Holland**
PUBLISHER **The Atlantic Monthly**
CATEGORY **Single Page/Spread**
DATE **July 1988**

PUBLICATION **Business Month**
ART DIRECTOR **Cynthia Friedman**
ILLUSTRATOR **Lane Smith**
PUBLISHER **Goldhirsh Group, Inc.**
CATEGORY **Single Page/Spread**
DATE **March 1988**

PUBLICATION **Regardies**
ART DIRECTOR **John Korpics**
DESIGNER **John Korpics**
ILLUSTRATOR **Alan E. Cober**
PUBLISHER **Regardies, Inc.**
CATEGORY **Story Presentation**
DATE **October 1988**

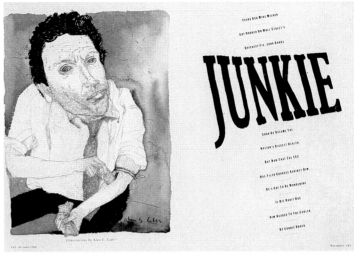

PUBLICATION **Sports Illustrated**
ART DIRECTOR **Steven Hoffman**
DESIGNER **Darrin Perry**
ILLUSTRATOR **Anita Kunz**
PUBLISHER **Time, Inc.**
CATEGORY **Story Presentation**
DATE **December 19, 1988**

PUBLICATION **Time**
ART DIRECTOR **Rudolph Hoglund**
ILLUSTRATOR **Mirko Ilic**
PHOTOGRAPHER **Roberto Brosan**
PUBLISHER **Time, Inc.**
CATEGORY **Cover**
DATE **September 1988**

PUBLICATION **Personal Finance Quarterly**
DESIGN DIRECTOR **Robert J. Warkulwiz**
ART DIRECTOR **William Smith**
DESIGNER **Michael Rogalski**
ILLUSTRATOR **Guy Billout**
CLIENT **Provident National Bank**
AGENCY **Warkulwiz Design Associates, Philadelphia, PA**
CATEGORY **Cover**
DATE **November 1988**

PUBLICATION **VPM - Veterinary Practice Mgt.**
DESIGN DIRECTOR **Bett McLean**
ART DIRECTOR **Deb Hardison, Lawrence Woodhull**
PHOTO EDITOR **Sara Elder**
PUBLISHER **Whittle Communications**
CATEGORY **Cover**
DATE **Winter 1988**

198

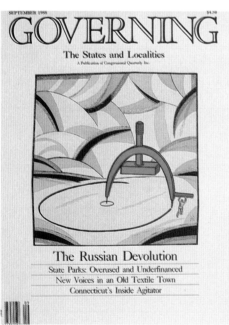

PUBLICATION **Governing**
ART DIRECTOR **Peggy Robertson**
ILLUSTRATOR **Brian Cronin**
PUBLISHER **Times Publishing Company**
CATEGORY **Cover**
DATE **September 1988**

PUBLICATION **Graphis**
ART DIRECTOR **B. Martin Pedersen**
DESIGNER **B. Martin Pedersen**
ILLUSTRATOR **Ven Verkaaik**
PUBLISHER **Graphis Publishing Corporation**
CATEGORY **Cover**
DATE **August 1988**

PUBLICATION **The New York Times Week in Review**
ART DIRECTOR **John Cayea**
ILLUSTRATOR **Mirko Ilic**
PUBLISHER **The New York Times**
CATEGORY **Cover**
DATE **February 28, 1988**

PUBLICATION **Tennessee Illustrated**
ART DIRECTOR **Mary Workman**
DESIGNER **Pam Smith**
ILLUSTRATOR **Phil Huling**
PUBLISHER **Whittle Communications**
CATEGORY **Single Page/Spread**
DATE **November/December 1988**

PUBLICATION **Fortune**
ART DIRECTOR **Margery Peters**
DESIGNER **Leo McCarthy**
ILLUSTRATOR **Brian Cronin**
PUBLISHER **Time, Inc.**
CATEGORY **Story Presentation**
DATE **July 4, 1988**

PUBLICATION **San Francisco Focus**
ART DIRECTOR **Matthew Drace**
DESIGNER **Matthew Drace**
ILLUSTRATOR **Lou Beach**
PUBLISHER **KQED, Inc.**
CATEGORY **Single Page/Spread**
DATE **August 1988**

PUBLICATION **GQ**
ART DIRECTOR **Robert Priest**
DESIGNER **Alejandro Gonzalez**
ILLUSTRATOR **Janet Woolley**
PUBLISHER **Condé Nast Publications, Inc.**
CATEGORY **Single Page/Spread**
DATE **November 1988**

PUBLICATION **San Francisco Focus**
ART DIRECTOR **Matthew Drace**
DESIGNER **Matthew Drace**
ILLUSTRATOR **Blair Drawson**
PUBLISHER **KQED, Inc.**
CATEGORY **Single Page/Spread**
DATE **January 1988**

200

PUBLICATION **GQ**
ART DIRECTOR **Robert Priest**
DESIGNER **Rhonda Rubinstein**
ILLUSTRATOR **Ian Pollock**
PUBLISHER **Condé Nast Publications, Inc**
CATEGORY **Single Page/Spread**
DATE **December 1988**

PUBLICATION **Premiere**
DESIGN DIRECTOR **Robert Best**
ART DIRECTOR **David Walters**
DESIGNER **Robert Best, MaryAnn Salvato, David Walters**
ILLUSTRATOR **Arnold Roth**
PUBLISHER **Murdoch**
CATEGORY **Single Page/Spread**
DATE **March 1988**

PUBLICATION **Sports Illustrated**
ART DIRECTOR **Steven Hoffman**
DESIGNER **Peter Herbert**
ILLUSTRATOR **Anthony Russo**
PUBLISHER **Time, Inc.**
CATEGORY **Single Page/Spread**
DATE **September 1988**

PUBLICATION **Consumer Electronics Monthly**
ART DIRECTOR **Daniel McDonald**
ILLUSTRATOR **David Frampton**
PUBLISHER **International Thomson Retail Press**
CATEGORY **Single Page/Spread**
DATE **December 1988**

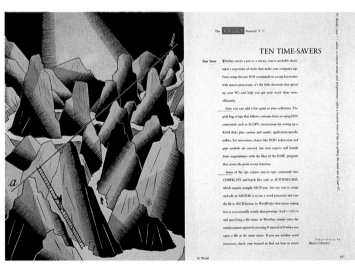

PUBLICATION **GQ**
ART DIRECTOR **Robert Priest**
DESIGNER **Rhonda Rubinstein**
ILLUSTRATOR **Julian Alllen**
PUBLISHER **Condé Nast Publications, Inc.**
CATEGORY **Single Page/Spread**
DATE **August 1988**

PUBLICATION **PC World**
ART DIRECTOR **David Armario**
DESIGNER **David Armario**
ILLUSTRATOR **Brian Cronin**
PUBLISHER **PCW Communications**
CATEGORY **Single Page/Spread**
DATE **January 1988**

PUBLICATION **Playboy**
ART DIRECTOR **Tom Staebler**
DESIGNER **Len Willis**
ILLUSTRATOR **Brad Holland**
PUBLISHER **Playboy**
CATEGORY **Single Page/Spread**
DATE **February 1988**

PUBLICATION **VLSI System Designs**
ART DIRECTOR **Sharon Anderson**
DESIGNER **Sharon Anderson**
ILLUSTRATOR **Patrick Blackwell**
PUBLISHER **CMP Publications**
CATEGORY **Single Page/Spread**
DATE **September 1988**

PUBLICATION **Rolling Stone**
ART DIRECTOR **Fred Woodward**
DESIGNER **Jolene Cuyler**
ILLUSTRATOR **Janet Woolley**
PUBLISHER **Straight Arrow Publishers**
CATEGORY **Single Page/Spread**
DATE **November 3, 1988**

PUBLICATION **Playboy**
ART DIRECTOR **Tom Staebler**
DESIGNER **Kerig Pope**
ILLUSTRATOR **Pat Andrea**
PUBLISHER **Playboy**
CATEGORY **Single Page/Spread**
DATE **December 1988**

PUBLICATION **PC Computing**
ART DIRECTOR **LLoyd Ziff, Jane Francis**
ILLUSTRATOR **Barbara Nessim**
CATEGORY **Single Page/Spread**
DATE **October 1988**

PUBLICATION **Rolling Stone**
ART DIRECTOR **Fred Woodward**
DESIGNER **Fred Woodward**
ILLUSTRATOR **Janet Woolley**
PUBLISHER **Straight Arrow Publishers**
CATEGORY **Single Page/Spread**
DATE **April 1988**

PUBLICATION **East/West Papers**
ART DIRECTOR **Jurek Wajdowicz**
DESIGNER **Jurek Wajdowicz**
ILLUSTRATOR **Andrzej Dudzinski**
CLIENT **The East/West Round Table**
AGENCY **Emerson, Wajdowicz Studios, NYC**
CATEGORY **Single Page/Spread**
DATE **May/June 1988**

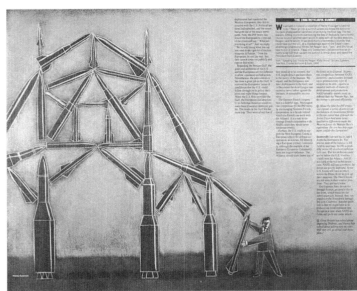

PUBLICATION **Rolling Stone**
ART DIRECTOR **Fred Woodward**
DESIGNER **Karen Simpson**
ILLUSTRATOR **Henrik Drescher**
PUBLISHER **Straight Arrow Publishers**
CATEGORY **Single Page/Spread**
DATE **March 24, 1988**

PUBLICATION **Security Management**
ART DIRECTOR **Roy Comiskey**
DESIGNER **Roy Comiskey**
ILLUSTRATOR **Matt Mahurin**
PUBLISHER **American Society for Industrial Security**
CATEGORY **Single Page/Spread**
DATE **May 1988**

PUBLICATION **Personal Finance Quarterly**
DESIGN DIRECTOR **Robert J. Warkulwiz**
ART DIRECTOR **William Smith**
DESIGNER **Michael Rogalski**
ILLUSTRATOR **Scott Reynolds**
CLIENT **Provident National Bank**
AGENCY **Warkulwiz Design Associates, Philadelphia, PA**
CATEGORY **Single Page/Spread**
DATE **November 1988**

PUBLICATION **MacWorld**
ART DIRECTOR **Christopher Burg**
DESIGNER **Christopher Burg**
ILLUSTRATOR **John Hersey**
PUBLISHER **PCW Communications**
CATEGORY **Single Page/Spread**
DATE **March 1988**

PUBLICATION **GSB Chicago**
ART DIRECTOR **Barb Rohm, Carol Gerhardt**
DESIGNER **Barb Rohm**
ILLUSTRATOR **Tom Curry**
CLIENT **University of Chicago**
AGENCY **Gerhardt & Clemons, Chicago, IL**
CATEGORY **Single Page/Spread**
DATE **Fall 1988**

Figure Likely Tax Hike Into 1988 Tax Planning

1987 Taxes:
Prepare Yourself

Autism:
The Prison
of Self

Aims and Aiming in Corporate Restructuring

Medical Ethics in History

From Athens to AIDS

Ethics and the Response to Plagues

Abigail Zuger, M.D.
Instructor in Medicine

PUBLICATION **The Stanford Magazine**
ART DIRECTOR **Andrew Danish**
DESIGNER **Andrew Danish**
ILLUSTRATOR **Greg Spalenka**
PUBLISHER **Stanford Alumni Association**
CATEGORY **Single Page/Spread**
DATE **Summer 1988**

PUBLICATION **NYU Physician**
ART DIRECTOR **Virginia Atkinson**
DESIGNER **Virginia Atkinson**
ILLUSTRATOR **Frances Jetter**
CLIENT **NYU Medical Center**
AGENCY **Virginia Atkinson Design & Co., South Norwalk, CT**
CATEGORY **Single Page/Spread**
DATE **Fall 1988**

PUBLICATION **The New York Times**
ART DIRECTOR **Jerelle Kraus**
DESIGNER **Jerelle Kraus**
ILLUSTRATOR **David Suter**
PUBLISHER **The New York Times**
CATEGORY **Single Page/Spread**
DATE **July 7, 1988**

PUBLICATION **The New York Times Week in Review**
ART DIRECTOR **John Cayea**
ILLUSTRATOR **Mirko Ilic**
PUBLISHER **The New York Times**
CATEGORY **Single Page/Spread**
DATE **February 28, 1988**

PUBLICATION **The New York Times Travel Section**
ART DIRECTOR **Michael Valenti**
DESIGNER **Michael Valenti**
ILLUSTRATOR **Anthony Russo**
PUBLISHER **The New York Times**
CATEGORY **Single Page/Spread**
DATE **November 11, 1988**

PUBLICATION **Access**
ART DIRECTOR **Byan Peterson**
DESIGNER **Bryan Peterson**
ILLUSTRATOR **Melissa Grimes**
CLIENT **Northern Telecom**
AGENCY **Peterson & Company, Dallas, TX**
CATEGORY **Story Presentation**
DATE **Fall 1988**

PUBLICATION **Vanity Fair**
ART DIRECTOR **Charles Churchward**
DESIGNER **Charles Churchward**
ILLUSTRATOR **David Hockney**
PHOTOGRAPHER **Helmut Newton**
PHOTO EDITOR **Elisabeth Biondi**
PUBLISHER **Condé Nast Publications, Inc.**
CATEGORY **Story Presentation**
DATE **June 1988**

PUBLICATION **Rolling Stone**
ART DIRECTOR **Fred Woodward**
DESIGNER **Jolene Cuyler**
ILLUSTRATOR **Nancy Stahl**
PUBLISHER **Straight Arrow Publishers**
CATEGORY **Single Page/Spread**
DATE **February 11, 1988**

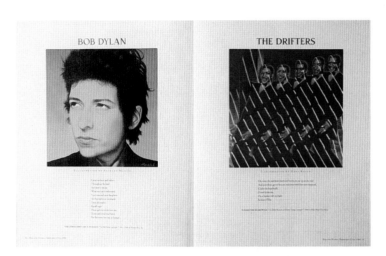

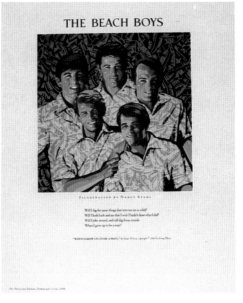

PUBLICATION **Rolling Stone**
ART DIRECTOR **Fred Woodward**
DESIGNER **Fred Woodward, Gail Anderson**
ILLUSTRATORS **Sean Earley, Robert Goldstrom, C.F. Payne, Brian Ajhar, Ian Pollack, Steve Pietzsch, Michael Witte, Anita Kunz**
PUBLISHER **Straight Arrow Publishers**
CATEGORY **Single Page/Spread**
DATE **February 1988**

OGRAPHY PHOTOGRAPHY PHOTOGRAP

24

► 24 A

► 24 B

PUBLICATION **Rolling Stone**
ART DIRECTOR **Fred Woodward**
DESIGNER **Jolene Cuyler**
PHOTOGRAPHER **Richard Avedon**
PHOTO EDITOR **Jim Franco**
PUBLISHER **Straight Arrow Publishers**
CATEGORY **Single Page/Spread**
DATE **April 7, 1988**

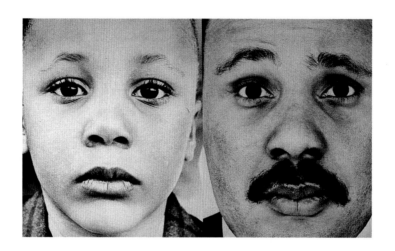

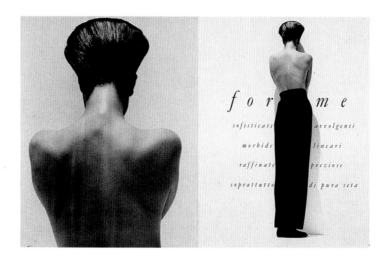

PUBLICATION **Italian Vogue**
ART DIRECTOR **Fabien Baron**
PHOTOGRAPHER **Herb Ritts**
PUBLISHER **Condé Nast International, Inc.**
CATEGORY **Single Page/Spread**
DATE **October 1988**

Gold

PUBLICATION **Arena**
ART DIRECTOR **Neville Brody**
DESIGNER **Neville Brody**
CATEGORY **Story Presentation**
DATE **Winter 1988**

PUBLICATION **Life**
ART DIRECTOR **Tom Bentkowski**
DESIGNER **Nora Sheehan**
PHOTOGRAPHER **Laurie Sparham**
PUBLISHER **Time, Inc.**
CATEGORY **Single Page/Spread**
DATE **April 1988**

212

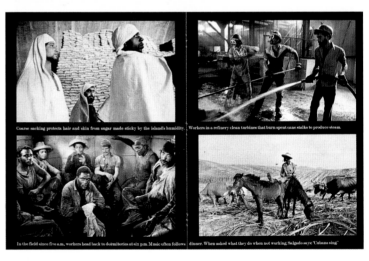

PUBLICATION **Life**
DESIGNER **Tom Bentkowski**
PHOTOGRAPHER **Sebastiao Salgado**
PHOTO EDITOR **Peter Howe**
PUBLISHER **Time, Inc.**
CATEGORY **Story Presentation**
DATE **August 1988**

Gold

PUBLICATION **Life**
DESIGNER **Robin Brown**
PHOTOGRAPHER **Mary Ellen Mark**
PHOTO EDITOR **Peter Howe**
PUBLISHER **Time, Inc.**
CATEGORY **Story Presentation**
DATE **June 1988**

214

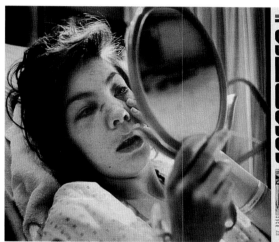

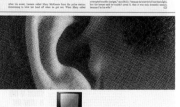

SPECIAL REPORT

STOP! FOR GOD'S SAKE STOP!

Four million women are beaten by their partners each year. In Minnesota, battered women are fighting back

'THE HOLD HE USED WAS TAUGHT IN VIETNAM. HE TOLD ME IT KILLS WITHOUT LEAVING MARKS'

'HE WAS SO SWEET. HE BOUGHT EACH OF MY DAUGHTERS A RED ROSE'

A 1984 STUDY SHOWED THAT ARREST IS THE MOST EFFECTIVE DETERRENT TO MEN WHO BATTER

'THE FEAR OF BEING BEATEN IS NOT AS STRONG AS THAT OF LOSING HIM'

PUBLICATION **Life**
DESIGNER **Tom Bentkowski**
PHOTOGRAPHER **Donna Ferrato**
PHOTO EDITOR **Peter Howe**
PUBLISHER **Time, Inc.**
CATEGORY **Story Presentation**
DATE **October 1988**

Gold

PUBLICATION **Viewpoint**
DESIGN DIRECTOR **Barbara Glauber**
ART DIRECTOR **Peter Deutsch**
PHOTOGRAPHER **Steve Hill**
CLIENT **Ernst & Whinney International**
AGENCY **Deutsch Design, Inc., NYC**
CATEGORY **Story Presentation**
DATE **March 1988**

Privatizing Public Services

Many U.S. state and local governments now contract out for public services. It's a good solution … but not for everyone, an E&W engagement finds.

by Stanley Ginsberg

Many levels of government in the U.S. now contract out for a variety of services formerly performed in-house. At left is Cynthia Regosich, a private court-security officer, shown in front of the Federal Courthouse in New York City. The fireman at right is Charles Herman, a firefighter with Rural/Metro Corp., a private fire company employed by the city of Scottsdale, Arizona.

The diversity of contracted services is vast. On the opposite

page is Lee Brown, a driver with Waste Management Co. of Phoenix, Arizona, with the company's standard one-man collection truck. On this page, standing, is Frank J. O'Connor, a public defender, in Redding, California.

Neither Black nor White

A Matter of Money

Parsons Municipal Services Inc. operates the nation's first privately built, owned, and operated wastewater treatment facility in Chandler, Arizona. Above, worker Rusty Rolfson is shown cleaning an empty clarifier; next page, bus driver Peter Manzano, of Tri-Camp Bus Lines, which handles municipal service in the Montclair, New Jersey, area.

Beyond Dollars and Cents

Stanley Ginsberg is a business journalist who frequently writes on public policy issues.

Every two hours the assembly line stops for 15 minutes and the workers break for tea or a card game. "It is a very human atmosphere. The factory is a part of their social life."

The steel plant, built in the 1930s, recently began to modernize. "It employs thousands of people. If it suddenly needs only 500, where are the rest of the workers going to go?"

A Zaporozhye steel plant worker, visored for protection against sparks, positions vats of molten ore. Says Salgado, "It's a dangerous profession. You have to concentrate all the time."

A TRIBUTE TO A VANISHING WAY OF
WORK

In a rare visit to Soviet factories, a photojournalist embarks on a labor of love

Sebastiao Salgado is in a race against time and technology. "There is an irreversible process taking place around the world, and it is happening faster than we think," says the 44-year-old photographer, speaking in the staccato bursts of a man in a hurry. "In ten or fifteen years, these pictures will be part of history." Salgado believes that computers and robots have delivered a "brutal shock" to the methods of production and "man no longer sees the fruits of his work." With missionary zeal, Salgado has begun to document the last vestige of a kind of labor that puts man in intimate contact with the product he creates. The photographs on the following pages, taken in a steel plant and an auto factory in Zaporozhye, a city of 863,000 in the Soviet Ukraine, are the initial dispatches of a three-year venture that will take Salgado around the globe. Future projects will include sugarcane fields in Cuba, chemical factories in West Germany, cotton fields in China, tin mines in Bolivia and limestone quarries in Indiana. "What I hope to achieve is a world portrait of a disappearing race, the working-class man," he says.

The son of a Brazilian cattle rancher, Salgado moved to Paris in 1969, where he earned a master's degree in economics. In 1973, as an economist for the International Coffee Organization in Africa, he found he was more interested in taking pictures than in filling out production reports. So he quit to make a career with a camera. "I could have photographed landscapes, but what interests me is something more basic and human. It is a struggle for dignity." In this, Salgado's images are in the tradition of W. Eugene Smith, the master of the photo essay, whom Salgado considers his major influence. "He had an enormous respect for people," says Salgado. Ten years ago Sebastiao visited a steel plant in France. The worker there "was strong; he had muscle; he was resistant," says Salgado. "Today it is an intellectual who makes steel." Indeed, a few weeks after he finished photographing at the Zaporozhye auto factory, the plant began installing robots.

119

PUBLICATION **Life**
DESIGNER **Tom Bentkowski**
PHOTOGRAPHER **Sebastiao Salgado**
PHOTO EDITOR **Peter Howe**
PUBLISHER **Time, Inc.**
CATEGORY **Story Presentation**
DATE **May 1988**

Silver

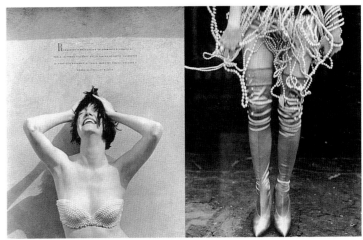

PUBLICATION **Italian Vogue**
ART DIRECTOR **Fabien Baron**
PHOTOGRAPHER **Steven Meisel**
PUBLISHER **Condé Nast International, Inc.**
CATEGORY **Story Presentation**
DATE **October 1988**

PUBLICATION **Italian Vogue**
ART DIRECTOR **Fabien Baron**
PHOTOGRAPHER **Steven Meisel**
PUBLISHER **Condé Nast International, Inc.**
CATEGORY **Story Presentation**

PUBLICATION **Sports Illustrated**
ART DIRECTOR **Steven Hoffman**
DESIGNER **Steven Hoffman, Peter Herbert**
PHOTOGRAPHER **Gregory Heisler**
PUBLISHER **Time, Inc.**
CATEGORY **Story Presentation**
DATE **April 25, 1988**

218

ALI
AND HIS ENTOURAGE

The champ and his followers were the greatest
show on earth, and then the show
ended. But life went on

Text by
GARY SMITH

Photographs by
GREGORY HEISLER

LANA SHABAZZ

FERDIE PACHECO

ALI'S STAFF

THE ENTOURAGE

THE WAR ZONE

PUBLICATION **Texas Monthly**
ART DIRECTOR **D.J. Stout**
DESIGNER **D.J. Stout**
PHOTOGRAPHER **Mary Ellen Mark**
PUBLISHER **Texas Monthly**
CATEGORY **Story Presentation**
DATE **November 1988**

PUBLICATION **Tucson Lifestyle**
ART DIRECTOR **Judith Byron**
DESIGNER **Judith Byron**
PHOTOGRAPHER **Steven Meckler**
PUBLISHER **Tucson Lifestyle Magazine**
CATEGORY **Cover**
DATE **August 1988**

PUBLICATION **Details**
ART DIRECTOR **Lesley Vinson**
DESIGNER **Lesley Vinson**
PHOTOGRAPHER **Stephane Sednaoui**
PUBLISHER **Advance Publishing Corporation**
CATEGORY **Cover**
DATE **June 1988**

PUBLICATION **Unisys**
ART DIRECTOR **Eric Madsen**
DESIGNER **Eric Madsen, Tim Sauer**
PHOTOGRAPHER **Kerry Peterson**
PHOTO EDITOR **Gary Teagarden**
CLIENT **Unisys Defense Systems**
AGENCY **Madsen & Kuenster, Minneapolis, MN**
CATEGORY **Cover**
DATE **Fall 1988**

PUBLICATION **The Boston Globe Magazine**
ART DIRECTOR **Lucy Bartholomay**
DESIGNER **Lucy Bartholomay**
PHOTOGRAPHER **Keith Jenkins**
PUBLISHER **The Boston Globe**
CATEGORY **Cover**
DATE **February 21, 1988**

PUBLICATION **The New York Times Magazine**
ART DIRECTOR **Janet Froelich**
DESIGNER **Janet Froelich**
PHOTOGRAPHER **Jeanne Strongin**
PUBLISHER **The New York Times**
CATEGORY **Cover**
DATE **September 18, 1988**

PUBLICATION **Stroll**
ART DIRECTOR **Melissa Feldman**
DESIGNER **Melissa Feldman**
PHOTOGRAPHER **Alexander Beck**
PUBLISHER **Stroll Magazine**
CATEGORY **Cover**
DATE **June 1988**

PUBLICATION **GQ**
ART DIRECTOR **Robert Priest**
DESIGNER **Robert Priest**
PHOTOGRAPHER **Sante D'Orazio**
PUBLISHER **Condé Nast Publications, Inc.**
CATEGORY **Single Page/Spread**
DATE **October 1988**

PUBLICATION **San Francisco Focus**
ART DIRECTOR **Matthew Drace**
DESIGNER **Matthew Drace**
PHOTOGRAPHER **Geof Kern**
PUBLISHER **KQED, Inc.**
CATEGORY **Single Page/Spread**
DATE **June 1988**

PUBLICATION **Life**
ART DIRECTOR **Tom Bentkowski**
DESIGNER **Tom Bentkowski**
PHOTOGRAPHER **Eugene Richards**
PHOTO EDITOR **Peter Howe**
PUBLISHER **Time, Inc.**
CATEGORY **Story Presentation**
DATE **July 1988**

PUBLICATION **Vanity Fair**
ART DIRECTOR **Charles Churchward**
DESIGNER **Charles Churchward**
PHOTOGRAPHER **Helmut Newton**
PHOTO EDITOR **Elisabeth Biondi**
PUBLISHER **Condé Nast Publications, Inc.**
CATEGORY **Single Page/Spread**
DATE **August 1988**

PUBLICATION **Vanity Fair**
ART DIRECTOR **Charles Churchward**
DESIGNER **Charles Churchward**
PHOTOGRAPHER **Helmut Newton**
PHOTO EDITOR **Elisabeth Biondi**
PUBLISHER **Condé Nast Publications, Inc.**
CATEGORY **Single Page/Spread**
DATE **July 1988**

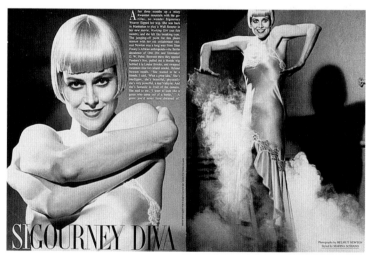

PUBLICATION **Vanity Fair**
ART DIRECTOR **Charles Churchward**
DESIGNER **Charles Churchward**
PHOTOGRAPHER **Helmut Newton**
PHOTO EDITOR **Elisabeth Biondi**
PUBLISHER **Condé Nast Publications, Inc.**
CATEGORY **Single Page/Spread**
DATE **June 1988**

PUBLICATION **Vanity Fair**
ART DIRECTOR **Charles Churchward**
DESIGNER **Charles Churchward**
PHOTOGRAPHER **Helmut Newton**
PHOTO EDITOR **Elisabeth Biondi**
PUBLISHER **Condé Nast Publications, Inc.**
CATEGORY **Single Page/Spread**
DATE **December 1988**

PUBLICATION **The Boston Globe Magazine**
ART DIRECTOR **Lucy Bartholomay**
DESIGNER **Lucy Bartholomay**
PHOTOGRAPHER **Keith Jenkins**
PUBLISHER **The Boston Globe**
CATEGORY **Single Page/Spread**
DATE **August 28, 1988**

PUBLICATION **The New York Times Magazine**
ART DIRECTOR **Janet Froelich**
DESIGNER **Nancy Harris**
PHOTOGRAPHER **William Wegman**
PHOTO EDITOR **Kathy Ryan**
PUBLISHER **The New York Times**
CATEGORY **Single Page/Spread**
DATE **December 1988**

PUBLICATION **GQ**
ART DIRECTOR **Robert Priest**
DESIGNER **Mark Danzig**
PHOTOGRAPHER **Matt Mahurin**
PUBLISHER **Condé Nast Publications, Inc.**
CATEGORY **Single Page/Spread**
DATE **August 1988**

PUBLICATION **Self**
ART DIRECTOR **Ken Kendrick**
DESIGNER **Izumi Inoue**
PHOTOGRAPHER **Kathryn Kleinman**
PUBLISHER **Condé Nast Publications, Inc.**
CATEGORY **Single Page/Spread**
DATE **December 1988**

PUBLICATION **Sports Illustrated**
ART DIRECTOR **Steven Hoffman**
DESIGNER **Darrin Perry**
PHOTOGRAPHER **Anthony Neste**
PUBLISHER **Time, Inc.**
CATEGORY **Single Page/Spread**
DATE **December 26, 1988**

PUBLICATION **Sports Illustrated**
ART DIRECTOR **Steven Hoffman**
DESIGNER **Steven Hoffman, Peter Herbert**
PHOTOGRAPHER **Gregory Heisler**
PUBLISHER **Time, Inc.**
CATEGORY **Single Page/Spread**
DATE **April 25, 1988**

PUBLICATION **Sports Illustrated**
ART DIRECTOR **Steven Hoffman**
DESIGNER **Darrin Perry**
PHOTOGRAPHER **Bruno Bade**
PUBLISHER **Time, Inc.**
CATEGORY **Single Page/Spread**
DATE **December 26, 1988**

PUBLICATION **Special Reports:Sports**
DESIGN DIRECTOR **Jim Darilek**
ART DIRECTOR **Michael Marcum**
DESIGNER **Ulrich Schendzielorz**
PHOTOGRAPHER **Salton Stall**
PUBLISHER **Whittle Communications**
CATEGORY **Single Page/Spread**
DATE **November 1988**

PUBLICATION **Rolling Stone**
ART DIRECTOR **Fred Woodward**
DESIGNER **Jolene Cuyler**
PHOTOGRAPHER **Herb Ritts**
PHOTO EDITOR **Laurie Kratochvil**
PUBLISHER **Straight Arrow Publishers**
CATEGORY **Single Page/Spread**
DATE **September 22, 1988**

PUBLICATION **Rolling Stone**
ART DIRECTOR **Fred Woodward**
DESIGNER **Jolene Cuyler**
PHOTOGRAPHER **Hiro**
PHOTO EDITOR **Laurie Kratochvil**
PUBLISHER **Straight Arrow Publishers**
CATEGORY **Single Page/Spread**
DATE **April 21, 1988**

PUBLICATION **Rolling Stone**
ART DIRECTOR **Fred Woodward**
DESIGNER **Fred Woodward**
PHOTOGRAPHER **Albert Watson**
PHOTO EDITOR **Laurie Kratochvil**
PUBLISHER **Straight Arrow Publishers**
CATEGORY **Single Page/Spread**
DATE **October 7, 1988**

PUBLICATION **Rolling Stone**
ART DIRECTOR **Fred Woodward**
DESIGNER **Gail Anderson**
PHOTOGRAPHER **Herb Ritts**
PHOTO EDITOR **Laurie Kratochvil**
PUBLISHER **Straight Arrow Publishers**
CATEGORY **Single Page/Spread**
DATE **June 30, 1988**

PUBLICATION **Rolling Stone**
ART DIRECTOR **Fred Woodward**
DESIGNER **Gail Anderson**
PHOTOGRAPHER **Matt Mahurin**
PHOTO EDITOR **Laurie Kratochvil**
PUBLISHER **Straight Arrow Publishers**
CATEGORY **Single Page/Spread**
DATE **October 6, 1988**

PUBLICATION **Rolling Stone**
ART DIRECTOR **Fred Woodward**
DESIGNER **Fred Woodward, Kathi Rota**
PHOTOGRAPHER **Matthew Rolston**
PHOTO EDITOR **Laurie Kratochvil**
PUBLISHER **Straight Arrow Publishers**
CATEGORY **Single Page/Spread**
DATE **June 16, 1988**

226

PUBLICATION **Rolling Stone**
ART DIRECTOR **Fred Woodward**
DESIGNER **Fred Woodward**
PHOTOGRAPHER **Kurt Markus**
PHOTO EDITOR **Laurie Kratochvil**
PUBLISHER **Straight Arrow Publishers**
CATEGORY **Single Page/Spread**
DATE **April 21, 1988**

PUBLICATION **Rolling Stone**
ART DIRECTOR **Fred Woodward**
DESIGNER **Jolene Cuyler**
PHOTOGRAPHER **Mary Ellen Mark**
PHOTO EDITOR **Laurie Kratochvil**
PUBLISHER **Straight Arrow Publishers**
CATEGORY **Single Page/Spread**
DATE **November 3, 1988**

PUBLICATION **Rolling Stone**
ART DIRECTOR **Fred Woodward**
DESIGNER **Fred Woodward**
PHOTOGRAPHER **Herb Ritts**
PHOTO EDITOR **Laurie Kratochvil**
PUBLISHER **Straight Arrow Publishers**
CATEGORY **Single Page/Spread**
DATE **March 24, 1988**

PUBLICATION **Rolling Stone**
ART DIRECTOR **Fred Woodward**
DESIGNER **Jolene Cuyler**
PHOTOGRAPHER **Herb Ritts**
PHOTO EDITOR **Laurie Kratochvil**
PUBLISHER **Straight Arrow Publishers**
CATEGORY **Story Presentation**
DATE **August 25, 1988**

PUBLICATION **Italian Vogue**
ART DIRECTOR **Fabien Baron**
PHOTOGRAPHER **Steven Meisel**
PUBLISHER **Condé Nast International, Inc.**
CATEGORY **Single Page/Spread**
DATE **November 1988**

PUBLICATION **Dateline**
ART DIRECTOR **Mitch Shostak**
DESIGNER **Anthony Kosner**
PHOTOGRAPHER **Bob Sacha**
CLIENT **American Express**
AGENCY **Shostak Design, NYC**
CATEGORY **Single Page/Spread**
DATE **November/December 1988**

PUBLICATION **Governing**
ART DIRECTOR **Peggy Robertson**
PHOTOGRAPHER **Scott M. Morgan**
PUBLISHER **Times Publishing Company**
CATEGORY **Single Page/Spread**
DATE **December 1988**

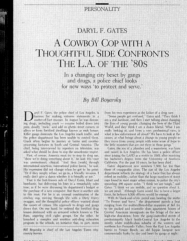

PUBLICATION **Physician Travel & Meeting Guide**
DESIGN DIRECTOR **Barrie Stern**
ART DIRECTOR **Georgina Sculco**
DESIGNER **Jo-Ann Osnoe**
PHOTOGRAPHER **Ric Ergenbright**
PUBLISHER **Cahners Publishing**
CATEGORY **Single Page/Spread**
DATE **May/June 1988**

PUBLICATION **VarBusiness**
DESIGN DIRECTOR **Joe McNeill**
ART DIRECTOR **David Loewy**
PHOTOGRAPHER **Danuta Otfinowski**
PUBLISHER **CMP Publications**
CATEGORY **Single Page/Spread**
DATE **October 1988**

PUBLICATION **Vanity Fair**
ART DIRECTOR **Charles Churchward**
DESIGNER **Charles Churchward**
PHOTOGRAPHER **Annie Leibovitz**
PHOTO EDITOR **Elisabeth Biondi**
PUBLISHER **Condé Nast Publications, Inc.**
CATEGORY **Story Presentation**
DATE **May 1988**

PUBLICATION **Vanity Fair**
ART DIRECTOR **Charles Churchward**
DESIGNER **Charles Churchward**
PHOTOGRAPHER **Annie Leibovitz**
PHOTO EDITOR **Elisabeth Biondi**
PUBLISHER **Condé Nast Publications, Inc.**
CATEGORY **Story Presentation**
DATE **March 1988**

PUBLICATION **Florida Magazine**
ART DIRECTOR **Santa Choplin**
DESIGNER **Santa Choplin**
PHOTOGRAPHER **Joe Burbank**
PUBLISHER **The Orlando Sentinel**
CATEGORY **Story Presentation**
DATE **August 1988**

PHOTOS BY JOE BURBANK

TOUGH LUCK

At one hard-nosed Florida facility, young men get a last chance to avoid prison, and a life of crime.

PUBLICATION **Life**
ART DIRECTOR **Tom Bentkowski**
DESIGNER **Robin Brown**
PHOTOGRAPHER **Harold Feinstein**
PHOTO EDITOR **Peter Howe**
PUBLISHER **Time, Inc.**
CATEGORY **Story Presentation**
DATE **August 1988**

PUBLICATION **Life**
ART DIRECTOR **Tom Bentkowski**
PHOTOGRAPHER **Koudelka, Nachtwey, Salgado, Jacobson,**
Peress, Singh,
PHOTO EDITOR **Peter Howe**
PUBLISHER **Time, Inc.**
CATEGORY **Story Presentation**

231

PUBLICATION **Life**
DESIGNER **Robin Brown**
PHOTOGRAPHER **Dilip Mehta**
PHOTO EDITOR **Peter Howe**
PUBLISHER **Time, Inc.**
CATEGORY **Story Presentation**
DATE **Spring 1988**

LIFE

BOOT CAMP

AN EXCLUSIVE LOOK INSIDE THE SOVIET ARMY BY ROY ROWAN

Photographs by James Nachtwey

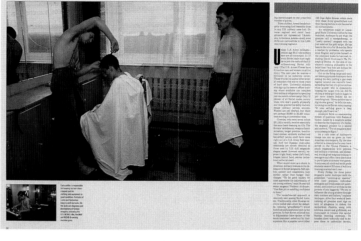

PUBLICATION **Life**
ART DIRECTOR **Tom Bentkowski**
DESIGNER **Robin E. Brown**
PHOTOGRAPHER **James Nachtwey**
PUBLISHER **Time, Inc.**
CATEGORY **Story Presentation**
DATE **November 1988**

PUBLICATION **Life**
ART DIRECTOR **Tom Bentkowski**
DESIGNER **Charles W. Pates**
PHOTOGRAPHER **Hiroji Kubota**
PHOTO EDITOR **Peter Howe**
PUBLISHER **Time, Inc.**
CATEGORY **Story Presentation**
DATE **September 1988**

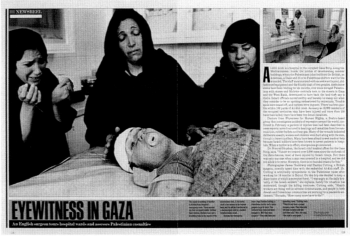

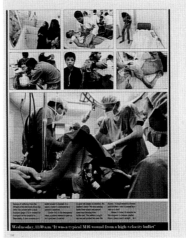

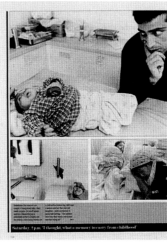

233

PUBLICATION **Life**
ART DIRECTOR **Tom Bentkowski**
DESIGNER **Tom Bentkowski**
PHOTOGRAPHER **James Nachtwey**
PUBLISHER **Time, Inc.**
CATEGORY **Story Presentation**
DATE **June 1988**

PUBLICATION **Life**
ART DIRECTOR **Tom Bentkowski**
DESIGNER **Marti Golon**
PHOTOGRAPHER **Joe Smoljan**
PHOTO EDITOR **Peter Howe**
PUBLISHER **Time, Inc.**
CATEGORY **Single Page/Spread**
DATE **July 1988**

234

PUBLICATION **Life**
ART DIRECTOR **Tom Bentkowski**
DESIGNER **Nora Sheehan**
PHOTOGRAPHER **Eric Valli**
PHOTO EDITOR **Peter Howe**
PUBLISHER **Time, Inc.**
CATEGORY **Story Presentation**
DATE **March 1988**

■ PICTURE ESSAY

They are our most public citizens, living and
dying before our eyes, but who are they?

BEGGARS

FRANCIS & LENA

Photographs Eugene Richards Reporting Edward Barnes

■ PORTFOLIO

A forbidden look at
the outcasts who are building
a highway 12,400 feet
in the sky

On the
Road

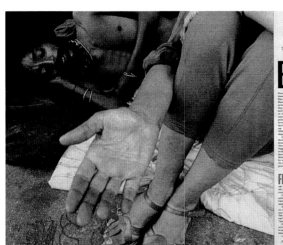

TOM

LINDA & MIKE

MARISOL

WADE

TO DAY
TARGET
ENDS

235

PUBLICATION **Life**
ART DIRECTOR **Tom Bentkowski**
DESIGNER **Robin Brown**
PHOTOGRAPHER **Eugene Richards**
PHOTO EDITOR **Peter Howe**
PUBLISHER **Time, Inc.**
CATEGORY **Story Presentation**
DATE **November 1988**

PUBLICATION **Detroit Monthly**
DESIGN DIRECTOR **Michael J. Ban**
ART DIRECTOR **Pamela Palms**
DESIGNER **Pamela Palms**
PHOTOGRAPHER **Michelle Andonian**
PHOTO EDITOR **Michelle Andonian**
PUBLISHER **Detroit Monthly**
CATEGORY **Story Presentation**
DATE **October 1988**

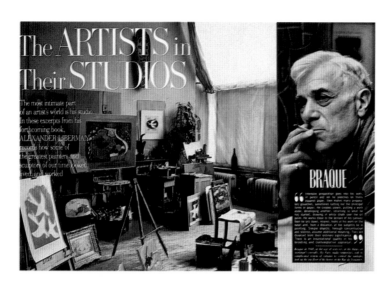

236

PUBLICATION **Vanity Fair**
ART DIRECTOR **Charles Churchward**
DESIGNER **Charles Churchward**
PHOTOGRAPHER **Herb Ritts, Alexander Liberman**
PHOTO EDITOR **Elisabeth Biondi**
PUBLISHER **Condé Nast Publications, Inc.**
CATEGORY **Story Presentation**
DATE **September 1988**

PUBLICATION **The Boston Globe Magazine**
ART DIRECTOR **Lucy Bartholomay**
DESIGNER **Lucy Bartholomay**
PHOTOGRAPHER **Keith Jenkins**
PUBLISHER **The Boston Globe**
CATEGORY **Story Presentation**
DATE **August 28, 1988**

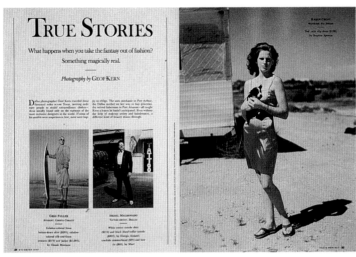

PUBLICATION **Texas Monthly**
ART DIRECTOR **D.J. Stout**
DESIGNER **D.J. Stout**
PHOTOGRAPHER **Geof Kern**
PUBLISHER **Texas Monthly**
CATEGORY **Story Presentation**
DATE **December 1988**

PUBLICATION **NYU Magazine**
ART DIRECTOR **Steven Hoffman**
DESIGNER **Steven Hoffman**
PHOTOGRAPHER **Peter Gregoire**
PUBLISHER **New York University**
CATEGORY **Story Presentation**
DATE **Fall 1988**

SAVE THE
VEGGIES

By Evan Eisenberg

Photographs by Sandi Fellman

Uncommon
Voices

238

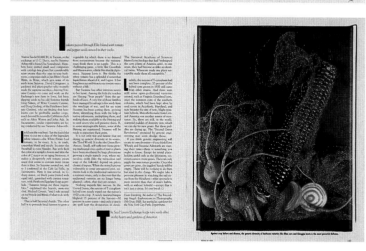

PUBLICATION **Connoisseur**
ART DIRECTOR **Sandra Di Pasqua**
DESIGNER **Sandra Di Pasqua**
PHOTOGRAPHER **Sandi Fellman**
PHOTO EDITOR **Phyllis Levine**
PUBLISHER **Hearst Corporation**
CATEGORY **Story Presentation**
DATE **March 1988**

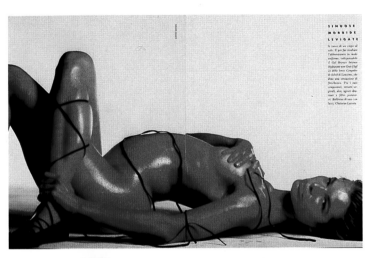

PUBLICATION **Italian Vogue**
ART DIRECTOR **Fabien Baron**
PHOTOGRAPHER **Steven Meisel**
PUBLISHER **Condé Nast International, Inc.**
CATEGORY **Story Presentation**
DATE **July 1988**

PUBLICATION **IQ**
ART DIRECTOR **MaryJane Fahey**
DESIGNER **MaryJane Fahey**
PHOTOGRAPHER **Mark Seliger**
PUBLISHER **CMP Publishing**
CATEGORY **Story Presentation**
DATE **December 1988**

WHERE ARE THEY NOW?

Catching up on a few of the many who have made a difference. Photography by Mark Seliger

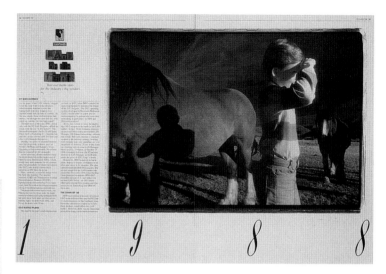

PUBLICATION **Lan Times**
ART DIRECTOR **Mike Christensen**
DESIGNER **Mike Christensen**
ILLUSTRATOR **Jean Arnold**
PHOTOGRAPHER **John Snyder**
PUBLISHER **Prolitho**
CATEGORY **Story Presentation**
DATE **December 1988**

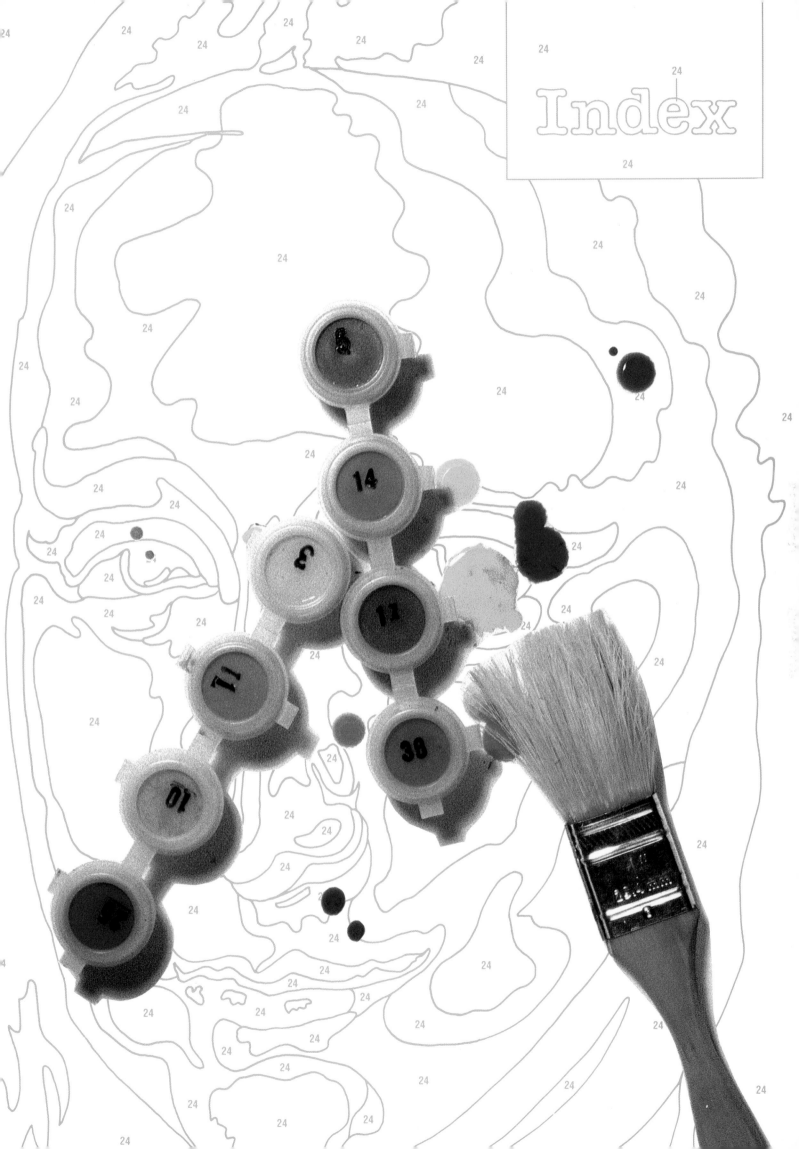

ART DIRECTORS INDEX

242

ILLUSTRATORS INDEX

PHOTO EDITORS

PUBLICATIONS INDEX

THE DEADLINE

SPEAKERS EVENINGS

Are held monthly and focus on the needs and common interests of the publishing industry. Noted designers, art directors, illustrators & photographers share their experiences through slides & discussions.

THE SPOT ILLUSTRATION COMPETITION

The SPOT illustration competition showcases the best SPOT illustrations in a publication, which communicate within a limited amount of space, a wealth of intelligence and style. The winners are exhibited in a two week show at the Art Directors Club of NY.

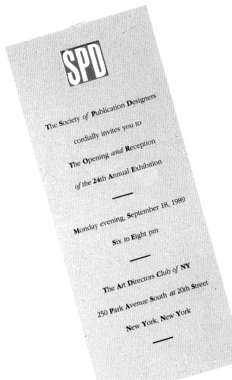

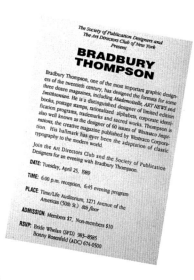